For Nancy
with loving wishes
for the best of
times!
Aunt Mary

CHANGE YOUR HANDWRITING
and
FEEL YOUR LIFE CHANGE

Mary Dawn Gladson

Forward by Phillip H. Taylor, M.D.

Published by Thoth, Inc., USA

First edition

Published by Thoth, Inc.
2533 N. Carson street No. 751
Carson City, Nv 89706

Original Cover painting by Carson Gladson

Library of Congress Catalog Card Number:
93-061801

ISBN 0-918993-53-9 (Hardcover)
ISBN 0-918993-54-7 (Softcover)

THE COVER PAINTING

Carson Gladson, Art Professor, El Camino Community College.

Some comments from art critics about Carson's work:

William Wilson, Los Angeles Times
"*He represents a type of rapidly disappearing artist and human being.*"

Thomas Albright, San Francisco Chronicle
"*They are interior paraphrases in language of highly introspective symbolism.*"

H. J. Weeks, Curator, Long Beach Museum of Art
"*These works maintain their interest to viewers over a span of time due to their strength and integrity.*"

> This painting was chosen as an image
> of feeling life becoming more beautiful.

Dedicated to

Biffy, my grandson

who devoted his three and one-half years
to living with exhuberant love and astonishing wisdom,
and to each one of my family.

ACKNOWLEDGMENTS

Please let me pay tribute to each one of you who has, knowingly or unknowingly, contributed to this project:

You individuals of diverse ages and walks of life, who have worked with me privately, validating these principles and inspiring the mandate to document them; the many thousands of you whose unique handwriting I have analyzed on Olvera Street, at the Renaissance Faire, and at private affairs; students and colleagues who have prodded me forward; Spencer Heath MacCallum whose assistance together with a scholarship from International Graphoanalysis Society made it possible for me to complete advanced studies, and who spent extended hours at the word processor; Norman Cousins who blew an encouraging breeze toward this effort that has often crossed the border of (to use his coinage) "self-tyranny;" Leanna Levy for her steadfast belief; Ralph Blum and Bronwyn Jones for their motivation and practical help; Gordon Stokes and Daniel Whiteside, who reignited the flame; my precious family, for their astute observations; dear friends for their enthusiasm and loyal urgings.

I would also like to acknowledge you who are about to begin your personal study. I look forward to the freedom you will feel as you sense your own many faceted selves coming true.

TABLE OF CONTENTS

FORWARD BY PHILLIP H. TAYLOR, M.D. PSYCHIATRIST
INTRODUCTION BY GORDON STOKES

CHAPTER TEN
INDEPENDENT THINKING AND PRIDE, TRUE OR FALSE

CHAPTER ELEVEN
DIRECTNESS (MIND ACTIVATING)

CHAPTER TWELVE

CHAPTER THIRTEEN

ALSO DISCUSSING:

CHAPTER FOURTEEN

CHAPTER FIFTEEN

CHAPTER SIXTEEN

CHAPTER SEVENTEEN
YOUR "r" AND "r"

ADDENDUMS

I was asked to read the manuscript for this book shortly before it went to press, to give the author an idea of the readability from a layman's point of view.

I found the book enticing and felt pulled through it from subject to subject.

The thing that frustrated me was having to remind myself that this was a manuscript and not my personal copy of the book. You see, I was constantly wanting to start practicing, right then!

Mark S. Gladson

Dr. Taylor is a physician with a specialty in Psychiatry. His approach is a biochemical–metabolic evaluation and treatment program.

He is a member of County and California Medical Associations, a director of the Los Angeles Psychodrama Center, a former president of the International Academy of Applied Nutrition and also holds membership in the American Academy of Environmental Medicine and the New York Academy of Science.

Forward

by Phillip H. Taylor, M.D. Psychiatrist

Handwriting analysis is being used by many businesses and professions in this country, and more extensively abroad.

Those using this method grasp the essence of professional-client understanding, and of personnel screening. Companies realize that one's personality traits and emotional makeup must fit job description, must point to adequate peer, and superior-subordinate relationships, must delineate an ability to advance and contribute to a company's success and well being. Key letters, their slants, strokes, rhythm, pressure, width and height are the fabric the handwriting analyst uses in constructing this psychological profile.

But this book is not of handwriting analysis. It is about an extension of this tool; an innovative and thought provoking approach; taking the basic precepts of handwriting analysis and using them as a tool for change - change in one's traits and emotional makeup.

In the field of psychotherapy this approach brings another choice to the seeker of change.

The concept of Mary Dawn Gladson is this: Learn the basics of handwriting analysis in her thorough, readable and interesting style, then apply it to yourself. Use it to revise facets of you by practicing the revised strokes.

This self-graphotherapy is thus born from the seed of handwriting analysis. Gladson highlights her writings with illustrations of those she has treated successfully in this manner. One might see oneself mirrored in some of these illustrations.

What does one need to read this book and perhaps apply it: an open mind, curiosity, thoughtfulness, close attention and an expectation of a healing of self.

INTRODUCTION

Symbols have been handed down through the centuries from all cultures to help communicate a thought or an idea. Handwriting is made up of symbols that represent what we wish to express.

In the brain, a place called Wernicke's area takes a major role in the written word and "heard" words, as well. To see a word is to pronounce it mentally. We see and feel it as colored by our emotional experience and our belief system. The same applies to the hands-on writing of words. When we read or write a word, its visual pattern is first perceived by the primary visual cortex, then transmitted to an area called the Gnostic (knowing) area. This area has to do with integrating past experiences - thoughts and feelings that have developed and accumulated through the years - with what is happening now. It's our way of learning to avoid painful experiences we've encountered from the past. So actions and decisions are not based on what is happening in the "Now," but a function of what has already happened.

The bottom line of all this is that the symbols that we use in handwriting reflect what we sense or feel. No wonder so many people hate even to sign their names.

When the mind is confused, the handwriting symbols show confusion. When the mind is muddled, the handwriting symbols indicate the same thing. As our feelings about ourselves change, the handwriting symbols change. So as we get better, it is reflected in our handwriting.

Now the brain does not know what is "real" or not. We build our own reality from what has happened in the past and how we feel about an experience. This is all reflected in our handwriting symbols. Now we can change our feelings and beliefs by working from the inside out, such as meditation, counseling, etc. We can also help to change from the outside in by exercise, change of diet or practicing a skill, as when we learned to type or ride a bicycle. We can make these changes even by consciously changing our handwriting.

Mary's book does both. It shows you how to change your focus from the inside out and you re-enforce this by consciously changing your handwriting. This records different symbols in the brain which signals to the brain that change is taking place. Once this skill becomes a habit, we can leave it to the body to respond differently - in a positive way - to the environment around us.

Can you understand the impact this can have on your life? We make choices in present time based on our experiences from the past. These choices we make in present time decide our future. Now if we can change the recorded images of the past by changing our handwriting, then we'll make different choices in present time that will give us a different future.

If you want to make positive changes now, put the information you find in this book to work. It's worth the small effort you'll do daily to prove to yourself that life can be beautiful.

Gordon Stokes
President
Three In One Concepts, Inc.

EXTRACT from *The Daily Breeze*, Torrance, California, Oct. 15, 1978
Staff writer, Jo Imlay

Expert believes handwriting tells all

Mrs. Gladson dishes out her service with tact, kindness and a sense of humor - even if she does know some things you wouldn't want your mother to find out.

"I've had a few surprises," she says with a laugh, launching into an anecdote.

"A man came to see me, and as soon as I looked at his writing, I knew there were many disturbances with him. It was difficult to know what to say, so I started with all of his good qualities."

The man grew increasingly edgy, obviously uncomfortable with any words of praise. Unable to listen any longer, he blurted out, "Do you know what I do for a living? I'm a professional thief."

That didn't daunt Mrs. Gladson.

"I smiled at him and said. 'You're probably a good one because you have excellent manual dexterity."

Her insights are sometimes surprisingly uncanny, even to her.

For instance, she studied one woman's handwriting and determined that she was intense and fond of rich experiences. Mrs. Gladson told her, "Life to you is like taking a can of orange juice concentrate and drinking it straight."

"Oh, I always drink my orange juice that way," the woman replied.

Another time she told a woman she ought to be a plumber, and-you guessed it-the woman was a plumber.

"It's fun when you hit things like that," says Mrs. Gladson.

"Change the handwriting, and you can change yourself," she says emphatically. . . "It takes practice, but you can use handwriting to bring out more desirable traits in yourself."

That's the advice she gives her young grandchildren, who often bring samples to her Los Angeles home when they visit.

Her children, however, are a bit more wary.

"My children say they don't want to write to me," she laughs.

After all, there are some things even one's own mother shouldn't know.

From the Publisher

This book is unique in that when you've finished with it, it will be uniquely yours. There will not be another book like this in the world. As you fill in the exercises it will reflect you and the changes you'll go through in order to increase your self-esteem, reopen your innate intelligence, augment your talents, reduce your stresses and expand your pleasure in everyday living.

_____

Your Signature

"Make it thy business to know thyself, which is the most difficult lesson in the world."

Miguel de Cervates

The familiar imperative, "Know thyself" has been ascribed to Plato, Pythagoras and Socrates. Juvenal says that this precept descended from heaven.

CHAPTER ONE
Feeling Your Life Change

Do you wonder about yourself? Why you feel the way you do? Why you act the way you do? Why people don't understand you? Why you don't understand them? Just who you are, anyway? Are you looking for answers?

- It's easier than you think.
- Look at your handwriting.

Are you wanting to get more out of life? To be your own free self?

That, too, is easier than you think.
Change your handwriting.

Our handwriting is a map of our total psychological makeup, our feelings, our fears, our needs, our aptitudes, our attitudes, our emotional nature, our mental capacities, our realities, our outlook on life. We can explore our every nook and cranny. We can be as we wish. We can live our life with pleasure.

Our writing, whether by hand, mouth, foot or mechanical substitute, is a true reflection of our emotional, mental and philosophical activity. It is a fossil record of our functioning at the time of writing. As Dr. Alfred Adler, the noted Viennese psychiatrist, expressed it, "Handwriting is frozen motion."

Every placement and movement of our pencil or pen is the result of our inner movement. Each dot, line, curve, loop, circle, hook and angle, has meaning, as have the size of the writing, the proportions of the structures, the slant, the heaviness and the spacing.

As our inner characteristics change, corresponding changes occur outwardly in our handwriting. Inner action precedes the outer. This is why we can change our handwriting and change ourselves. As we consciously repeat specific outer action, we necessarily reiterate specific inner action thereby acquiring the behavioral habits we choose.

We can come alive. We can sense our own balanced, integrated selves, freed of any psychological fears, escapes and resistances.

We can meet life, day by day, with intelligence and joy.

From infancy we are confronted with aspects of a world that are frightening. We develop psychological fears. Some of the fears we find in our handwriting are:

Fear of DISAPPROVAL
　Fear of making DECISIONS
　　Fear of our EMOTIONS
　　　Fear of FAILURE
　　　　Fear of GIVING
　　　　　Fear of being INSECURE
　　　　　　Fear of not being LOVED
　　　　　　　Fear of not being PERFECT
　　　　　　　Fear of REALITY
　　　　　　　　Fear of RIDICULE
　　　　　　　　　Fear of RELATIONSHIPS
　　　　　　　　　　Fear of SUBJUGATION
　　　　　　　　　　　Fear of the UNKNOWN

With each fear we automatically find ways to resist or escape whatever it is we fear. Some of the psychological resistances and escapes seen in the handwriting are:

ABUSE of others and self
　AGGRESSIVE BEHAVIOR
　　DECEIVING others
　　DECEIVING ourselves
　　　DEFIANCE of authority
　　　　DOMINEERING others
　　　　DAYDREAMING
　　　　　EXAGGERATED IMAGINATION
　　　　　FATIGUE
　　　　　　MANIPULATING others
　　　　　　POSSESSIVENESS
　　　　　　PROCRASTINATION
　　　　　　　REPRESSED EMOTIONS
　　　　　　　RESENTMENT
　　　　　　　RIGIDITY
　　　　　　　　SECRETIVENESS
　　　　　　　　SELFISHNESS
　　　　　　　　　STUBBORNNESS

TEMPER
SHALLOW GOALS
VANITY
WANDERLUST

We attack or flee because we have abandoned our innate resources for doing otherwise. When our inner strengths diminish, fears, resistances and escapes take hold. We put ourselves at the mercy of the world. We react compulsively. On the other hand, when we own our individuality, we realize there is nothing to fear. We need neither to fight nor to run away. We act from choice.

The healthier we are psychologically, the less affected we are by the assaults and batterings of everyday living. Psychological health depends upon the strength of inner balance and absence of fear. These characteristics manifest themselves in the same way in every handwriting. Consequently, as you go through this program, you will find that there are ways in which your handwriting will come to resemble that of any other well-balanced individual.

You may ask, "Doesn't this lessen my individuality?" The opposite is true. Your individuality is sharpened, its vulnerability reduced.

The healthier our bodies, the less susceptible they are to illness. Physical health depends upon the healthy functioning of the various components of the body.

Just as a healthy heart and healthy lungs are some of the indicators of a healthy body, there are certain indicators in our handwriting of our psychological health. These, naturally, evidence themselves in the same manner in the handwriting of each person.

As you follow this program, the fine qualities of your special personality, your unique talents and capabilities, will become more clearly defined and facile. You will become free to be who you are, prepared to meet your challenges and achieve your desires.

You will find that your flow of energy will be more consistent, and that you will have greater wisdom in using it productively.

While this program does not guarantee material success, it will equip you with the tools to help you achieve any goal. It does not guarantee you will never know sadness and hurt, but as your sense of personal integrity prevails, you can be aware, even more, of a current of inner joy that flows beneath discomfort. You can make intelligent and joyful living a daily experience.

Norman Cousins, in his books, *Anatomy of an Illness* and *The Healing Heart*, builds a vivid case for the role wholesome emotions play in our health. In a later book, Human Options, he goes on to say that "The evidence is incontrovertible that chemical changes take place in the body as a result of mental functions or moods." During the hours spent with Norman Cousins he was delightful and receptive. His encouragement sent me toward the publishing of this book with accelerated enthusiasm. I'm grateful to him. Since the daily use of self-graphotherapy makes it possible to create and maintain a secure emotional and mental state, it is an important aid to health.

I acknowledge this to be a sample of my handwriting — with apologies to your eyestrain, Norman Cousins

This original approach is thorough and complete. It is founded on this principle: When our natural innate strengths are in tact and operating, when we build and maintain our inherent, full-faceted inner potency, we can dissolve our accumulated psychological fears. And along with them, our escapes and resistances, that caused us to behave regrettably and drive us into self bondage, can be dissolved. We can be free to act and think in accord with our own personal integrity.

The conclusions presented in this book are the outcome of my experiences with the many thousands of people whose handwriting I have analyzed, among whom are those many people of diverse ages and life situations who have worked privately with me.

In the Appendix there are many "real life" samples of handwriting containing numerous variations and combinations of traits. However some of the illustrations demonstrating certain characteristics have necessarily been manufactured, so may appear drawn, unnatural. Changing basic elements in one's personality can be difficult, and uncomfortable. This is an important reason why forgeries can be detected, and why these underlying aspects, as explained in Chapter Two, are not arbitrarily altered.

The casual observer tends to believe that similar behavior is prompted by similar motivation. Each writing shows a different pattern of traits and reveals the different motivations behind individual behavior. This study shows you how to distinguish for yourself.

SELF-GRAPHOTHERAPY WORKS!
Because it works it is essential to start at the beginning. If you skip through the chapters, selecting the traits that are most appealing to you, you may experience disap-

pointment and discomfort. *Attempting to rid yourself of your fears, escapes and resistances prematurely could leave you feeling defenseless, as if the rug had been pulled out from under you. Building strong drives before you know where you want to direct them could be detrimental to your well being and to your success. Systematic procedure is the sure and expeditious way.*

Provided you follow the sequence, traits may be added as rapidly as you can achieve them. The balance you discover through your exercises in Chapter Three is the cornerstone of your integrated personality and is vital to successful progress. Without your inner balance other traits can work to your disadvantage.

PENCILS AND PAPER ARE THE ONLY MATERIALS YOU NEED. Softer lead pencils (#2 usually works well) let you see more clearly the variations in pressure, width or heaviness of your writing. The lead submits readily to the energy you exert. Unlined paper is better because it does not restrict the formation, size and line of your writing.

Mary Dawn Gladson

P.S.

You might find it entertaining to chronicle particular events as they occur and observe the manner in which you deal with them as related to the changes you have made in your handwriting.

> *"Yet more enduring are you than the earth, than the sun and all the spheres in the heavens. All shall pass away but you shall not. Why tremble you as leaves in the wind?"*
>
> *Mikhail Naimy*

CHAPTER TWO
Common Basic Characteristics.

here are certain basic elements in every personality, ingredients that are common to us all:

Our emotional make-up
  • The speed with which we respond emotionally
  • The depth of our emotional experiences
Our Rhythm
Our Concentration

EMOTIONAL SPEED is identified by the slant of our writing.

I know this is a sample of my handwriting

I know this is a sample of my handwriting

I know this is a sample of my handwriting

This is a sample of my handwriting

EMOTIONAL DEPTH, by the heaviness or pressure of writing.

pressure pressure pressure
pressure pressure pressure
varied in one writing

RHYTHM, by the consistency of the line of writing; the baseline.

baseline baseline baseline
baseline baseline baseline
baseline baseline baseline

CONCENTRATION, by the size of the writing

concentration and size of writing
large to small the degree
of concentration can vary
in one sample of writing

These four underlying basic characteristics, emotional speed, depth, rhythm and concentration, adjust themselves. They do not need to be changed arbitrarily. They will do this of their own accord, as a natural outcome of your self-discovery, as you re-establish or increase the inner strength you need to dispense with the psychological fears that have caused these traits to operate undesirably. A conscious change at this time could cause discomfort.

It will be helpful, however, to recognize these aspects of your personality and understand how your behavior is affected by them, and the part they can play in relationships. They can be a major factor in compatibility.

You can begin recognizing characteristics in your handwriting by using the space provided for a sample of your personal writing. Please write freely in your usual manner. First write: "I acknowledge this is a sample of my handwriting." Then talk about what changes you would like to have happen in your life, and sign your name. Please fill the page.

My Personal Handwriting

1. SLANT (Emotional Speed)
   - Does your writing slant to the right?
   - To the left?
   - Is it perpendicular?
   - Does the slant vary?

2. DEPTH OR PRESSURE (Emotional Depth)
   - Is your writing heavy?
   - Is it light?
   - Is it moderate?
   - Does it vary?

3. LINE OF WRITING, Base-line (Rhythm)
   - Is it straight?
   - Does it move upward?
   - Does it move downward?
   - Does it vary?

4. SIZE OF WRITING (Concentration)
   - Is it very large?
   - Is it very small?
   - Is it medium size?
   - Does it vary in size?

These individual basic traits have an overall effect upon each other and upon all other traits. Other traits can alter the manner in which these traits are manifested. The following four elements are described as if they were unaffected by any other characteristic in the personality.

THE SLANT OF YOUR WRITING AND YOUR EMOTIONAL SPEED

You have your own inner emotional behavior, which can be very different from what you exhibit outwardly. Your inner emotional behavior has two components, the speed of your emotional response to your environment, and the depth of your emotional experience. Opposite emotional structures are often a factor in compatibility.

Your emotional speed is the speed with which you, within yourself, feel your emotions go into action--how fast you respond emotionally to any stimulus. It is not **what** you are feeling - anger, love, jealousy, compassion, but how fast you are feeling it. This is your inner reaction, not necessarily your outward expression.

The speed of your emotional response has nothing to do with the depth of your feelings. Speed is indicated by the slant of your writing; this relationship may seem obvious, and it is. When your writing slants forward, to the right, it shows greater speed, the farther right, the faster the rate of speed.

handwriting

handwriting

The degree to which your writing slants to the right the more likely it is that you:

- Are not afraid to let your emotions come alive.
- Are always emotionally awake.
- Can feel the emotional tug to behave impulsively.
- Are inwardly involved on-the-spot, although you may not show it. You also may not be able to hide it.
- Direct yourself toward the world, not yourself.
- Look ahead rather than behind.
- Feel ready to crusade for your beliefs.
- Can usually move fast, and speed up your schedule.

Even though you may feel an immediate surge of emotion you may appear to be the quintessence of calm. You can also feel excited and show it. In any case, your emotions impel you toward your environment, even though protective traits can restrict your outward movement.

my handwriting.

If your handwriting rises perpendicularly there is no speed; you are in neutral, emotionally standing still; consequently you often find that you:

- Feel little or nothing at the moment a stimulus is presented.
- Can experience a delayed emotional response to stimuli.
- May not be able to laugh or cry, or express any emotion, as readily as some others.
- Can, under the pressure of emotional build-up, feel like exploding for little or no immediate reason.
- Need to feel safe, secure, emotionally and in all ways.
- Weigh all matters on your inner emotional scale.
- Think how you, personally, will be affected by an action before you consider taking it.
- Do not like to be, and often cannot be, hurried.
- Need to plan for emergencies or you may be late for an appointment.

- May be able to deal with emergencies because your emotions are not immediately involved.

With a perpendicular slant you can also give the impression of being excited when you are not feeling it. You can, at times, find it difficult to pretend. You can appear uninterested because you are unable to share or experience a feeling at a moment's notice. To compensate, you may become unusually active socially, or you may limit yourself socially.

If you write with a perpendicular, or very slight right slant, you are attempting to escape from your own emotional response to an environment that may harm you if you allow yourself to be affected by it. Your fear invites self-centeredness.

If your writing slants leftward it is plain to see that your

speed is in reverse; you are spontaneously withdrawing.

You find that you:
- Are in emotional reverse, backing away from stimuli.
- Feel threatened by the world, even when you want to be involved in it.
- Are very self-protective, even if you are service oriented.
- Want what will support your personal needs.
- Are afraid to direct yourself emotionally toward anyone but yourself.
- Find it difficult to relate closely with anyone, but can also cling to a trusted one.
- Can behave extraordinarily sociably to compensate, and may prefer relating with a wide variety of people.

A left slant shows you are running away from your emotions and your environment, emotionally retreating, even when being outwardly active.

The degree to which your slant is perpendicular or leftward, indicates the degree of your fear of emotional insecurity, of the inner demand for any kind of personal security. Your fear causes you to become centered toward your own self; you want to be certain your self-involvement will not turn out to be your undoing. The fear that causes writing to be perpendicular or slant to the left, or slightly to the right, can begin at a very early age. When a child's emotions seem unacceptable or are denied, the only way the child can find to control emotional expression is not to feel anything, to retreat within to a safe emotional distance. And now you continue to consider your own personal security before and above all else.

handwriting

If your writing slants only slightly to the right, You are responding slightly emotionally, but not so much so that you can't keep both feet on base.

handwriting

If your writing slants a bit farther right, you are responding somewhat more emotionally, but you are keeping one emotional foot on base. You don't feel like going, nor do you feel like staying. You're pulling yourself both ways.

Some experience the entire range of emotional speed, from extremely fast to medium, to slight, to none, to going in reverse. With such variation, your writing runs the gamut from left to right.

handwriting

If your slant varies from left to right and back again, the speed of your emotions is changing accordingly. It can vary hour to hour or minute to minute.

Consequently:
- You don't know what to expect of yourself--nor do others know what to expect of you.
- You can feel excited one minute and the next, feel nothing
- You can identify with feelings of others more easily than they can with yours.
- You likely feel more satisfied with different kinds of activities than you do confined to a particular one.

- You can greet people in a friendly manner one time and at another time find it difficult even to muster "Hello."

If your slant is consistently to the right or to the left; if it is consistently perpendicular; if it is consistently a slight or moderate one, you know what inner emotional speed to expect of yourself. You can make allowances. You can anticipate your reaction because you know how your emotions will affect you, so you can prepare in advance.

If, on the other hand, your slant changes rapidly throughout the day it is difficult for you to compensate; you don't know how to prepare for situations because you don't know how you're going to feel.

Understanding characteristics represented by your slant, depth, line and size of writing helps you to understand yourself and others. You can recognize some of the reasons why compatibility is easier in some relationships than in others.

THE DEPTH OR PRESSURE OF YOUR WRITING AND YOUR EMOTIONAL DEPTH

The other aspect of your underlying emotional makeup is found in the depth of your writing, in the pressure you exert on your writing instrument as it meets the paper.

Some of us write with very heavy pressure, some with very light pressure, some with moderate pressure or any gradation in between. Some of us have pressures that vary from one extreme to the other. Handwriting can vary in pressure as well as in slant.

When you examine the heaviness, pressure or depth of your writing you can find some answers to the following questions:

- How deeply do emotional experiences impress you?
- How long do they last?
- How much energy do you have?
- Do you have strong likes and dislikes?
- How sensitive are you to color, sounds, smells, texture or tastes?
- Do you remember feelings others forget?
- Do you forget feelings others remember?

- Do you bore easily?
- Does your energy wax and wane?
- Does your interest wax and wane?

Heavy Pressure

If your pressure is heavy your emotional experiences penetrate your being and last a long time, perhaps forever. Some say they can remember back to their birth. Prompted by a fragrance or a sound you are catapulted back in time to smells, sounds, colors and feelings of earlier experiences, so that you relive them.

Very heavy writing sometimes clogging

If your writing is extremely heavy:
- Your feelings are intense.
- You are extremely sensitive to color, fragrance, sounds, tastes, textures.
- Your sensuous demands can be so strong as to override reason.
- You can find it difficult to break a habit.
- Emotional attachments are binding, making it painful to release them.
- You can form opinions based on prejudice, if you have not developed traits to counter this bias.
- You can have an over-abundance of energy that must be expended wisely, physically, mentally and emotionally, or you can either exhaust yourself from over-doing, or be tired from the sheer weight of unburned fuel.
- You are saturated with the sum (total) of your emotional experiences, your likes and dislikes, pains and pleasures.

very light pressure

pencil barely floats

over paper

Light Pressure

Extremely light pressure indicates the opposite of all that is over-abundant in extremely heavy writing.

- Emotional experiences tap at your heart, while the heart of the very heavy writer is bludgeoned.
- Emotional experiences touch only the surface of your feelings and fade.
- You have little energy, emotional, mental and physical.
- You can keep busy to avoid boredom, not because you have the energy or particular intense interest.
- You can be tired for no reason.
- You can be bored even when circumstances are to your liking.
- You can have only a mild response to color, fragrance, tastes; your likes and dislikes are not deeply imbedded.
- You may have a good mental memory, for time, dates and locations, but your emotional, or sensuous memory is short-lived.
- You are afraid to deal with your emotional experiences so you blow them quickly away, as you would a dandelion puff.

When you discharge your emotional experiences, you simultaneously discharge your energy and your interest. You are not deeply enough involved in a subject to build up energy toward it, or an interest in it, so you become tired and bored.

Our pressure can vary
even within words

When your pressure varies from heavy to light you are in constant mental conflict. You have no idea how you're going to handle your emotions. They have you in a quandary. Your feelings, your energy, your interest, your sensitivity waxes and wanes unpredictably.

the slant and pressure both vary making us unpredictable to both ourselves and others

When both your speed and your pressure are varied you never know what any of your emotional reactions will be, nor does anyone else. You are constantly threatened by the discomfort of this unmanageable fluctuation of energy, interest and aesthetic sensitivity.

steady strong pressure

With consistently strong pressure, not excessively heavy or light, you can meet the world with an energetic handshake, not crushing its hand nor letting yours lie limply within it. Your pencil doesn't float lightly on the paper, nor does it imprint several pages beneath.

- You maintain interest in projects and have the energy to handle them.
- You are not compulsively driven toward, or away from, them.
- You are sensuously touched by fragrance, sound, texture, taste, but your senses do not control you.
- You are emotionally loyal, but when your intelligence advises you that it is necessary, you can release an attachment, even when it hurts.

To repeat, all traits must be evaluated with all other traits.

YOUR LINE OF WRITING AND YOUR RHYTHM

Rhythm, as seen through handwriting, has to do with consistent, overall mental and emotional outlook.

Rhythm can be seen most readily in the line, or the Base-line of your writing. Your line of writing reveals your inner attitude of optimism and pessimism.

- Does your line of writing, or your Base-line, move upward?
- Does it move downward?
- Does it move both up and down?
- Does it move in an even straight line?

If your line of writing moves generally upward you have a general feeling of optimism. You see the silver lining behind every cloud. You feel tomorrow will be better. No matter what happens, the world cannot keep you down.

If your line of writing moves generally downward, you have a general feeling of pessimism. Things are going wrong and they always will, and you can do nothing about it.

If your Base-line moves up and down, sometimes frequently even within words, in an irregular manner, it is obvious that your inner attitudes are fluctuating in the same manner: "Life's good, life's bad, life's good, life's bad".

As with a varied slant and varied pressure, you don't know what to expect your attitude to be: You can usually roll with the punches, because you are constantly rolling inside yourself.

If your Base-line is even and regular you are aware of an inner sense of rhythm that keeps you moving smoothly from thought to thought, action to action, as if on a well laid track. You maintain an even-keeled outlook on life.

If your line of writing is precisely regular, you can find that unexpected jolts, surprises, sometimes even pleasant ones, disturb you. With very even writing a pebble on your track can feel like a boulder.

If your Base-line, along with your slant, pressure and size are very regular, it is difficult for you to take the ups and downs of life.

Your line of writing may move generally upward or generally downward and also have an even Base-line. This indicates that you have even rhythm and also maintain an attitude of looking on either the bright or dark side.

Different rhythms between you and another can cause misunderstanding, unless you learn to recognize what is happening within yourself and the other person.

To repeat, you are not attempting to achieve precision in these aspects of your writing. The basic elements explained in this chapter will adjust themselves, if necessary, of their own accord. You need not be concerned if they seem unmanageable at this time.

THE SIZE OF YOUR WRITING AND HABITUAL CONCENTRATION (INTENSITY OF YOUR FOCUS)

If the middle zone of your writing is one-sixteenth of an inch or less in height, you possess the trait of concentration, of habitual, unavoidable concentration. You leave yourself no alternative but to concentrate. You concentrate by compulsion, not by choice.

When your lower case letters are one sixteenth of an inch or less in height your concentration has become a psychological escape, as is light pressure and a perpendicular or left slant.

- You concentrate to escape from a world that might push its way into your own personal, private inner sphere.
- You have the capacity to focus tightly upon one thing, but you also lose your selectivity about the subject of your focus.
- Wherever your attention lights is where it remains until it is drawn elsewhere, or until you make the effort to tear it away.

- You can become distracted.
- You can go to the store for a paper and come back with a doughnut.
- You may drive your car and walk home. It is not your memory, but distraction due to the change of focus of your concentration.
- Sudden interruptions can be disconcerting, can give you a strong inner jolt.
- You may need to be called several times before you hear the call.

Concentration magnifies every other characteristic. All other traits become stronger in proportion to the intensity of your habitual concentration.

If your writing is particularly large, it is due to your desire to avoid focusing upon a specific area.

The size of your writing can vary as can your slant, pressure and rhythm.

In Summary

Your emotional responsiveness you see in your slant; the depth of your emotions you see in your pressure; your rhythm you see in the line of your writing; your concentration you see in the size of your writing; all are elemental in your total personality, and have a global effect.

These basic factors, through this system of self graphotherapy, take care of themselves. If it is to your benefit, they will change of their own accord. The essential, initial step in productive change comes in the next chapter.

As you restore your inner strength and vanquish your psychological fears and conflicts these major characteristics will assume the constructive roles they are designed to play within your integrated complete self.

Make no conscious effort to alter them. To force such a drastic change could result in discomfort. When they change progressively your comfort grows.

Integration begins with your first exercise.

Following this chapter are pages of actual handwritings that demonstrate a variety of slants, pressures, base-lines, and sizes of writing.

This is a sample of my handwriting.

This is a sample of my handwriting

This is a sample of my handwriting

This is a sample my handwriting

y handwriting

This is a sample of my handwriting

this is a sample handwriting

This is a sas hand writing

my handwriting

This is a sample of my handwriting

handwriting is a sample handwriting

this is a sample handwriting

This is a sample my handwriting.

my Handwriting

This is a Sample of my
Handwriting

is a Sample

is a sample

my handwriting

is a sample

is a Sample

This is a sample of
my handwriting

This is a sample of
my handwriting

This is a sample of
my handwriting

This is a sample
my handwriting

is a sample

is a sample

is a sample

is a sample

is a sample

is a Sample

is a sample

is a Sample

my handwriting my me

my handwriting is a sample

my handwriting is a sample

my handwriting is a sample

my handwriting is a sample

my handwriting is a sample

my handwriting is a sample

my handwriting is a sample

my Handwriting is a sample

my handwriting is a Sample

my handwriting is a sample

my handwriting is a sample

my handwriting is a sample

CONVERSATIONS SUGGESTING COMPATABILITY CHALLENGES

Can you relate to the following conversations? Differences in slant, pressure, size of writing, baseline, perspective, and other characteristics can cause discord in relationships and elicit conversations that may go something like these:

She: *I never know what's going on with you. This morning you were all gung-ho about going out tonight, and now you say you have to work. I can't figure you out.*

He: Well, Jack's plane was late so I had to give that talk at the breakfast meeting. Then I had to play racquet ball with a client. After that I hurried across town to see that new car you liked. When I got back I found my secretary was out sick and no one had called a temp, then after the board meeting.....

She: *Why can't you ever keep your mind on one thing? You're always doing fifteen things at once. I can't stand it when you do that.*

He: I know you can't. If one little thing doesn't go the way you planned, you think the world's falling apart.

He: Did you call Anne?

She: *No, I...*

He: You said you would call her.

She: *I know, but...*

He: Why didn't you? I told Jim you'd call her.

She: *She called me before I.....*

He: And you didn't tell her about the invitation?

She: *Yes, I told her . It's all taken care of.*

He: Well, you should have called her.

He: Are you about ready? We should be there by now.

She: *Don't rush me.*

He: Why are you always late? No matter what time we set for leaving, you're never ready.

She: *If I didn't always have all these things coming up at the last minute I'd be on time too.*

He: You never want to stay at home.

She: *And you never want to go anyplace.*

He: But you've been out all day. And now you want to go visit the Jones who live a half-hour away?

She: *Yes, that'll be better than watching some old movie. I know, why don't we plan a trip?*

He: A trip? We just got back.

She: *I know, but....let's go to.....oh, I know, the South Seas!*

He: Can't we just relax, build a fire, and watch that old movie? I'll go to the corner and get a new one if you want it.

She: *I'll go with you and then we can go on to.....*

She: *You always look on the dark side.*

He: And you're a Pollyanna.

She: *I'm not. I just know we can find a way out.*

He: That is not a practical point of view.

He: You don't remember our most sentimental times. You don't even remember that magnificent sunset, purple and gold and pink and orange...and the brisk breeze, and the smell of those trees in bloom...the dampness curled your hair, you didn't like it, but you looked so pretty.

She: *I remember something you don't, the date. It was April 11, 1984. What's so important about remembering the color of the sky? You make such a big deal about some things and totally forget others, like my birthday. You're always either late or early.*

He: Well, I remember what I want to get you. I saw this smooth satin nightgown, and there was a soft, snuggly blue robe. I can just see you in it.

(She comes in the door)

She: *Where's Carrie?*

He: What do you mean? Isn't she with you?

She: *Didn't you pick her up from the baby sitter?*

He: No, was I supposed to?

She: *Yes, I told you this morning when you were shaving, that I'd be late, and you'd have to pick her up.*

He: Oh, I guess I didn't hear you . I'll go right now.

She: *I don't know where your mind goes sometimes.*

She: *You were certainly quiet tonight. What's the matter, don't you like the Williams?*

He: I like them, a lot. I just didn't have anything to say. The conversation was lively without me.

She: *You should enter in more. People will think you don't like them.*

He: I invited them here. Anyway, you're friendly enough for both of us.

She: *That's not the point.*

"Make thy mind thy Kaaba,
Thy body its enclosing temple,
Conscience its Prime Teacher".
      Kabir

"Poetic Justice, with her lifted scale,
Where in nice balance truth with gold she weighs,
And solid pudding against empty praise".
      Alexander Pope

CHAPTER THREE
Balance

The Cornerstone of your Strength

Balance gives strength. Strength conquers fear. It nullifies the need to struggle frantically with demands of your environment. It invigorates.

The cornerstone of your impregnable inner power is your personal inner balance, the harmonious interplay of your mind, body and conscience (spirit). As you coordinate your inner tri-functioning you feel a sense of inner equanimity that counteracts the effect of conflicts and pressures. It helps you deal with a volatile world without being violated by it.

Balance is absolutely essential to practical, intelligent functioning in your everyday life, to eliminating your psychological fears that can thrust you into fighting against and/or escaping from the world and yourself. Without balance you reduce the possibility of joyful, intelligent living, you restrict your experiences and the free flow of mental, emotional and physical energy. To live satisfyingly, you need to experience equally and simultaneously, your entire tri-being, body, mind, and spirit. No isolated part of yourself can function fully and healthily without the support of the others.

The three dimensions of yourself are:
1 - The mental, mundane, everyday, intellectual, communication.
2 - The concrete, material, tangible, known, physical, people.
3 - The abstract, intangible, unknown, philosophical, conscience, spirit.

Corresponding to your three dimensions are three zones or areas in your handwriting:

1 - The middle zone (mental)
2 - The lower Zone (concrete)
3 - The upper Zone (abstract)

Upper zone

Middle zone

Lower zone

hug bog sky

The upper zone is the area penetrated by structures, namely, the loops of your lower case *h,k,* and *b,* that extend above the middle zone which rests on the baseline.

The middle zone contains the humps of *h,* and *k,* and the circle part of the *b;* also lower case vowels and *r,s,m,n,v,u,x,* etc; and those parts of *g,y,z,q,* and *j* that do not extend below the baseline.

The lower area or zone is found in those structures that do extend below the baseline.

THE LOWER ZONE, the concrete area:

"The body is the tool of the human spirit--a beloved and respected tool, the edge of which should not be dulled"----
Spencer Heath

young

zing

queque

jinx

This area represents the tangible, material world, having to do with people, money, things, with concrete matters. It indicates the emphasis we place on physical and material desires, needs and possessions. The structures you write in this lower zone indicate your individual interest in, and need for, the physical, material, people aspects of life, and the kind of attention you direct toward them.

In attempting to perceive and discuss your tri-dimensional self the body is easiest to describe. You can see it, touch it, smell it. You know when it hurts, when it feels good, when it is sick and when it is well. Your body can perform physical feats. It can both work and play. Each organ, bone, muscle, and nerve has a name and can be located. With your physical senses you can observe and contact the physical world of people, places and things.

Observe Your Handwriting

Please use this page for a sample of your handwriting and observe the structures that are illustrated and explained in this chapter. Write free-flow, without copying or writing something from memory. Use additional paper if necessary to accommodate your ideas and/or the size of your writing.

My Personal Handwriting

An explanation of how the written structure relates specifically to the physical body is superfluous in this discussion, except to note that the body, inasmuch as it houses both the mental and abstract dimensions, is portrayed throughout all three zones.

The Mind is less obvious than the body. However, the brain is a well known component of the body. Those who are equipped to do so have investigated it quite thoroughly and understand many of its intricacies. Without any knowledge of the workings of your brain you know what you are thinking, and there are those who specialize in evaluating mental efficiency. So we do have resources that can assist in describing the mind. Given there is much yet to be known about the brain, there is much that has been discovered. Now and then the mind asserts, "I can do it by myself," but when all is said and done, it knows it cannot perform in this physical world without the body.

THE MIDDLE ZONE, The mental Area

". . . . the mind is restless, turbulent, strong and unyielding. . . as difficult to subdue as the wind."
Bhagavad-Gita

This area reveals mainly your mental processes and the manner in which you communicate. It is the area of everyday, mundane functioning. It represents the manner in which you think your way throughout day-to-day living. The mind collects information, processes it, stores it, decides how to act upon it and to communicate it. The mind also can build upon information, adding fact to fact and thought to thought.

You can manifest these thoughts in concrete ways, such as in a physical structure, a culinary creation, in teaching, in business, in mechanics, in being with people, in keeping a household, in a work of art. The mind can work inventively in solving problems and developing products.

Your abstract dimension is far more difficult to describe. You cannot see it, touch it, or contact it through your senses or your mind. No amount of exploratory surgery can locate it. Your mind, with the use of your complicated brain, cannot probe into or comprehend your third dimension. Your mind can, however, understand that this vital, intangible element of your being is necessary to your sense of inner peace. It can realize how the acceptance of the concept of the unknown works toward your personal and practical successes.

When your innate inner consciousness is given permission it will automatically assist your mind in its day-to-day intelligent functioning.

When your mind refuses to accept your inner consciousness, your philosophical self, it is because it is afraid of learning something it doesn't want to know.

THE UPPER ZONE, The Abstract Area

"...to know that what is impenetrable to us really exists, manifesting itself as the highest wisdom and the most radiant beauty..."

..Albert Einstein

THE ONLY structures we consider as abstract structures are the upper extenders of *h, k, b,* and *f*. Other strokes or structures such as t and d, while they may reach above the middle zone, do not apply to the abstract consciousness. Observe ONLY *h, k,* and *b*. The f will be considered in Chapter Four.

The abstract area is the area of the unknown; the philosophical. This is the intangible, third dimension of our being, that which the body cannot sense, nor the mind invade. The mind can, however, reject it, either totally or partially.

The upper loops of your *h, k,* and *b,* represent your inner consciousness, an intellectually indefinable awareness that allows you to function beyond the limitations of your everyday concerns. This abstract capacity is essential to your practical, intelligent daily living. You may tend to neglect this part of yourself more than any other.

With full use of this area you can keep each moment, each day, each year in perspective with all of life. You can put problems and situations in perspective. Without it you cannot; they become larger than life. Your mind can over-emphasize them, and fail to see their context.

When you are aware of your intangible self you have the desire and the capacity to discover ultimate truth, the meaning of life itself. You have your own personal sense of conscience, your philosophical code, that is not dependent upon the whimsical moralities and expediencies of the world. You can perceive yourself and life as a whole. You no longer feel fragmented, incomplete. You can understand how to put pain and pleasure into perspective.

Your abstract dimension allows you to set major goals, because you can be aware of all of your options, not only those presented by a world that is less capable of seeing them. This inner awareness helps build and direct your self-confidence, enthusiasm, your energy, toward magnetizing goals. You can look beyond the immediate to plan long-range.

Without your abstract inner consciousness, your mind can become submissive to the senses and to material demands. It can be enticed to choose the shadow and ignore the substance.

These three areas of your being, vital to your comfortable survival, are so diverse you might well ask, "How can they co-exist in one entity?"

They can live together harmoniously when each is given full recognition and credence. No one of the three can work at its best alone; each needs the other two. Your body needs your mind to instruct it. Your mind needs your body to house it. Your spirit needs your mind to apply it. Your everyday life can be enjoyed fully when the three components of your being are integrated-- when they operate in proper proportion to one another.

Your initial effort in self-graphotherapy is to understand your tri-self, to establish or renew your inner balance, your personal coordinated functioning.

You do this by bringing your physical, mental and philosophical parts of your being into present time, into everyday reality.

The primary step in finding your strength:

The baseline of your handwriting represents your individual, practical, everyday reality. If you are to use your resources to gain your inner power, your body, mind and spirit must connect with this, your own, day-to-day reality.

Proportion among your three areas, as represented in the three zones of your handwriting, is determined by actual measurement. To find the proper proportions in your writing begin by:

LOCATING YOUR BASELINE

First, write (do not print) words, phrases or sentences that contain all zones of writing, such as:

hang king bang handwriting baking cooking bungle hiking bring hinge hooking huge

---

My Personal Handwriting

Printing confines you to a prescribed, limiting structure, thus confining your psychological, mental, physical, abstract, emotional being. It can be used as a disguise

Now, draw a line along the bottom of the middle zone of each letter, starting at its first "foot" (identified in the drawing by a single asterisk) to its last foot (double asterisk). This gives each structure, or letter, its particular baseline. These short lines join to form a continuous line that is your baseline.

Your baseline may be straight and even, or it may rise and fall with all manner and frequency of ups and downs. Nevertheless, it is your baseline and represents your everyday, mundane reality.

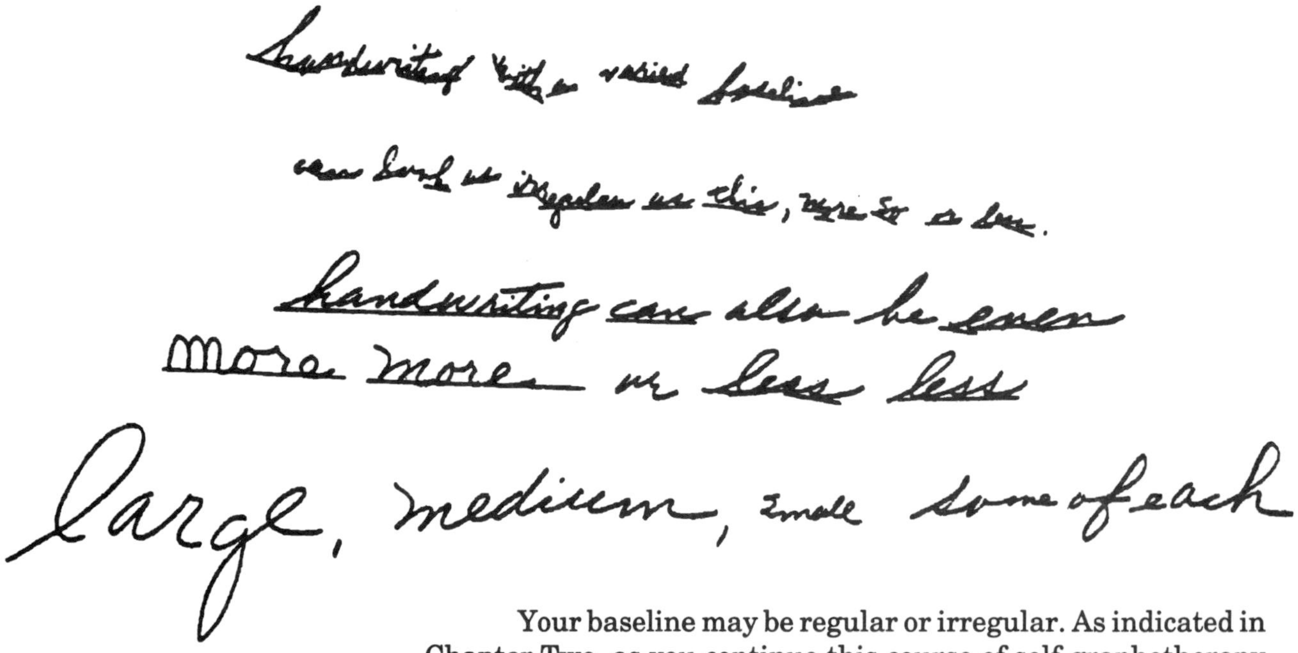

[handwriting sample: "handwriting with a varied baseline"]

[handwriting sample: "can be as irregular as this, more so or less."]

[handwriting sample: "handwriting can also be even"]

[handwriting sample: "more more or less less"]

[handwriting sample: "large, medium, small some of each"]

Your baseline may be regular or irregular. As indicated in Chapter Two, as you continue this course of self-graphotherapy your baseline may change naturally if it is to your benefit for this to happen.

DETERMINING YOUR MIDDLE ZONE

To locate the middle zone, the mundane, mental area, draw a line or lines along the tops of your lower-case, middle-zone, letters or structures.

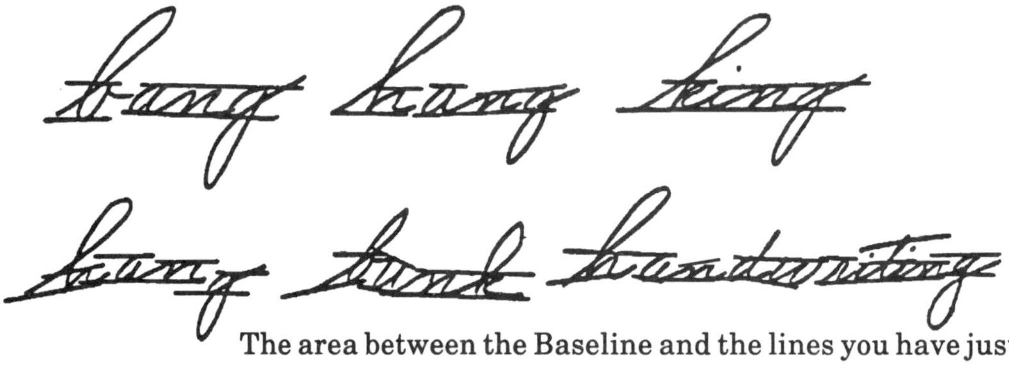

[handwriting samples with lines drawn]

The area between the Baseline and the lines you have just drawn is the middle zone. The shapes, of your letters and the regularity of your writing are not factors in determining your middle-zone, which is your mundane or mental area.

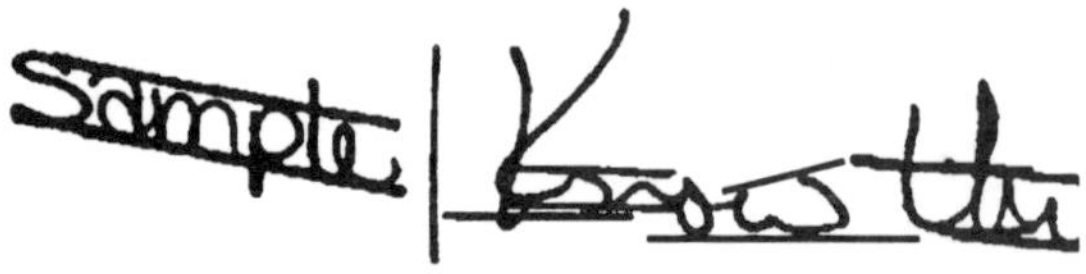

If we allow our minds to be omnipotent we cannot envision further than the fleeting present. Temporary security becomes our only security. We are afraid of the unknown, of anything more than we can see before our eyes. Even when we have the self-confidence to challenge our talents, if we cannot accept the unseen, the undiscernible, as a given quantity we cannot deal realistically and practically with the here and now, with daily, mundane goals that can lead toward our ultimate ones.

So we move on to the abstract area which helps the mind to function more intelligently.

DETERMINING YOUR UPPER ZONE

Having established the height of your middle zone, you can now measure the height of your upper zone. Your abstract capacity is found in the loops of *h*, *k*, and *b* that extend above the middle zone of the letter. Look ONLY at *h*, *k*, and *b*. (IGNORE *d* and *t*, *d* and *t* do not apply to the abstract capacity). The letter *l* is an abstract loop, but you do not to attend to it except under a circumstance that will be mentioned later.

The upper loops of your *h*, *k*, and *b* must measure two-and-a-half to three times the height of the middle-zone of the letter. These loops must also be the same width as that of the hump in your *h* and *k*, or the circle part of your *b*. This provides a consistently workable proportion between the mental and the abstract.

Consider the middle zone of *h*, *k*, *b* as one unit.

The upper zone (loops) must be 2 1/2 to 3 units higher than the middle zone (1 unit).

The loops must also be the same width as the width of the

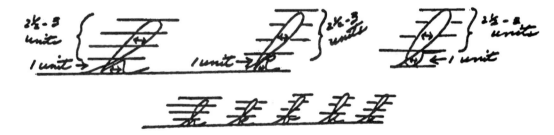

middle zone.

As in the demonstration following, you:

1 - Begin the up stroke of the loop at the baseline which signifies everyday existence, your day-to-day reality.

2 - The stroke moves up from the baseline into the upper zone, forms a smooth-flowing loop of proportionate width as it comes back down to the baseline, thus bringing your abstract consciousness into use in your daily functioning.

3 - The structure continues as you move upward to form the middle zone (the hump or circle) of the letter, and return to the baseline.

4 - To complete the letter/structure, extend your final stroke forward to the right.

ELIMINATED UPSTROKE

NARROW LOOP

LOOP TOO SHORT

IF YOUR LOOP is narrower than the middle zone of the letter but is in proportionate height, or if you eliminate the up stroke, retaining only a single-line down-stroke, you are restricting the use of your individual abstract consciousness in proportion to the restriction of the loop. This is evidence that you are limiting your abstract imagination and your intelligent functioning.

IF YOUR LOOP is too short to qualify for the proportionate height, you are being dependent upon your environment for your philosophical point of view. You are not penetrating your own abstract being; you are unaware of your own inner consciousness. Your mind is glued tightly to the everyday, limited consciousness of mundane thought and activity--a sign of limited intelligent functioning.

Lacking your own philosophical concepts, you tend to accept or reject those of others at face value without the verification of your own individual conscience, even though you may have formed intellectual conclusions. You can submit to the world's fluctuating social/ethical standards and behavior and adjust your philosophical code in order to get what you want in the physical world.

If your upper stroke is very short, it can be due to a reluctance to grow up, to accept adulthood and mature responsibility. You limit your ability to see the overall picture of life, of yourself and of your projects. You limit your ability to define your major goals and to make plans to achieve them. The immediate looms large. You cannot put situations in perspective. Minor problems can become major.

IF YOUR LOOP is wider than the width of the middle zone of the letter, your abstract imagination is, more or less, exaggerated. It's vitality is diluted. The wider the loop grows, the broader the imagination and the leniency of philosophical concepts. If the loop is twice or more the width of the lower part of the letter, your abstract capacity loses its resiliency. Your inner consciousness is ballooning to accommodate behavior in yourself and others that you would otherwise find unacceptable. Your innate concept of ultimate reality has lost its focus.

If your abstract loops do not start at the baseline and return to the baseline, you are not relating your philosophical nature realistically to your thinking and the actions of everyday life.

When you do not use your abstract ability, your mental processes are forced to carry a heavy burden, a burden for which they are not equipped. To function intelligently they need the influence of your vitally important abstract nature that allows your mind to consent to the idea of the existence of an unknown quantity in life and in yourself.

When your philosophical, or upper, zone is mis-proportioned your mental, emotional, physical compulsions can rule you. Your conscious choices can be invalid. With your consistent, proportionate use of your abstract nature, you have your own individual point of reference for every thought, decision and action, not one determined by fluctuating public perception.

Your abstract ability automatically eliminates an energy-wasting and stress causing trait that we call "defiance of authority."

DEFIANCE OF AUTHORITY:

Indicated when the abstract loop and the hump or buckle, of the letter k are out of proportion. The Middle Zone of the k extends higher than the other middle zone structures, partially and sometimes totally eliminating the philosophical area. You can also see "defiance of authority" when k (as well as any other letter) is printed to replace the usual lower case formation.

Many people develop this trait. It is a psychological resistance to any person or situation you feel might try to wield authority over you or restrict your freedom in any way. It does not represent a rational point of view; it is, rather, a compulsion and can even become a paranoid-type attitude in regard to real or imagined authority. This fear of subjugation can begin at a young age.

With "defiance of authority" you can find yourself thinking, "I'm my own boss! Don't you dare tell me what to do!" Such an attitude can cause muscular tension, tightness in the neck, shoulders, back, etc.

Even though you developed this trait "legitimately," as a protection against imposed authority, "defiance of authority" is not in your best interest. It can cause you to "cut off your nose to spite your face." You can resist authority that does not exist. You are misdirecting and wasting your energy in fighting your real or imagined enemy instead of meeting it intelligently with a productive use of your energy.

Practice Assignment

You can feel something happening in you with your first exercise. Write the letters *h, k,* and *b* many times, over and over. Follow the demonstration with upper loops in proper proportion to the middle zone, starting at the baseline and returning to the baseline. Some may find this easy, some more difficult. Remember, ***proportion is natural***. It is innate within you. Disproportion comes because you have allowed your environment to pull you away from your own true self. Practice until results seem natural.

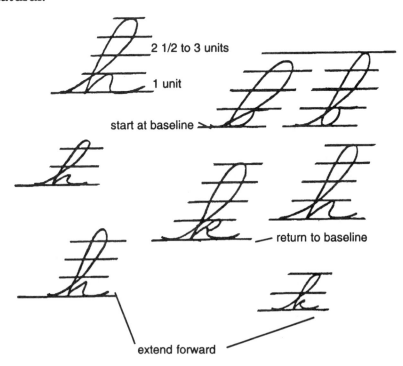

These upper loops represent your innate inner knowledge, knowledge with which you were born. The most extensive study of philosophies cannot give you this.

Your capacity to be aware of your inner consciousness, of the abstract, the unknown, is essential if you are to deal constructively with every aspect of your concrete, material world.

This physical, and people, area of activity is found in your lower zone of writing, in the strokes extending below your baseline.

DETERMINING YOUR LOWER ZONE

As is demonstrated below, to establish the proper proportionate size of these lower loops, follow the same pattern that you did for the upper loops. The length of the lower loops of the letters *g, y, z* and *q* must be two-and-one-half to three times as long as the height of the middle-zone of the letter; the width of the loops must be the same width as that of the middle-zone.

The down stroke of the loop leaves the middle zone of the letter at the baseline. It extends down to the proper length, forms a smooth loop with proportionate width, as it moves back up to cross the down stroke at the baseline, thus bringing the physical aspects of your being and life into practical, everyday reality.

Upper and lower loops, the abstract and the material, are approximately the same, with allowance for modest variations in the middle zone. This does not apply to the letter *p*. The lower structure of the letter *p*, has individual characteristics that are not presently considered.

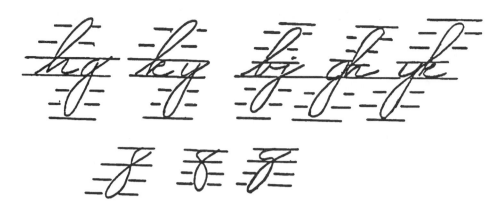

Also, you may form your letter *g* in a manner similar to the *figure 8*, as in the above illustrations, and those to follow.

This is the trait of fluidity of thought, which many literary people have acquired. It is necessary to adhere to the proper proportion, even though the shape is different from the usual formation of the letter.

As you achieve this proportionate functioning in the physical area, a number of non-constructive traits automatically vanish. These include the following:

EXAGGERATED IMAGINATION:

Indicated by lower loops that are wider than the middle zone of the letter. The wider the loop, the more exaggerated the imagination.

Exaggerated imagination can cause you to create a mountain from a molehill, or from nothing at all, or to relate an event inaccurately without realizing it. You manufacture "facts" that do not exist. You might form compulsive, even indiscriminate, associations with people.

You can feel an obsessive need for variety and demanding desires for money and things.

You may be able to relate more easily with many people than you can on a one-to-one basis; or you can be demanding of one who you feel can satisfy your needs.

This trait plus the trait of self-deceit, discussed in Chapter Six, often add up to feelings of paranoia. Information is added or subtracted according to the psychological need to escape the reality you fear, so you deny its existence. You manufacture a pseudo reality which is even more frightening.

Another trait you eliminate when your lower zone, your material area, is in proportion, is <u>need for change</u>.

NEED FOR CHANGE:
Indicated by lower extenders that are longer than three times the height of the middle zone.

This length, when added to the wide loops of exaggerated imagination indicate a restlessness that can be irresistible.

"The grass is greener. . ;" "I feel like flying the coop;" "I have to get out of here!, take a trip, go away". This is a psychological escape, a demand for both change and variety. If you see this in your writing you are dwelling on material elements which pull your mind off course and drag it down into the quicksand of the purely physical. It moves from "here" to "there," from "thing" to "thing," person to person. With this compelling psychological restlessness, logical, intelligent choice is lost; any place can seem better than where you are, any *thing* better than what you have. One of anything is hardly enough. Nothing specific, no matter how greatly desired, brings lasting satisfaction. The restlessness, itself, creates another desire.

With excessively long lower extenders, your determination to achieve material goals calls for an unreasonable amount of energy--a misuse of this precious resource.

With the above formations of your lower loops you can be compulsive about people relationships. You can, on the other hand, be afraid of relationships and limit them compulsively. This fear has risen because you, in some way, have been hurt or disappointed in relationships.

LIMITED SELECTIVITY IN RELATIONSHIPS:

Indicated by lower loops that are narrower than the width of the middle zone.

If this shows in your writing you select your relationships, not by your intelligent choice, but as a psychological escape from the world of people, any of whom you feel could hurt you.

'LONER' ATTITUDE:

Indicated by lower extenders that have no loops. With this trait you are psychologically escaping intimate closeness with anyone, unless experience has taught you to trust a certain person. You feel safest in relationship with yourself, even if you are emotionally outgoing, deeply loving and sentimental.

CLANNISHNESS:

Indicated by lower loops that do not return to cross the down stroke at the baseline.

This feeling of clannishness also limits your relationships by psychological escape, running away from people in general for fear one or some of them may bring you sorrow, dislike you, shun or discard you. You need to be assured that there is some common denominator with another that will make you acceptable to that person who will remain loyal to you.

As the loop gets smaller and crosses farther away from the baseline, the need to escape into a sometimes possessive, totally secure, safe relationship grows stronger. Fear overrules intelligent choice.

DISCOMFORT IN PAST RELATIONSHIPS:

Indicated by lower loops that are distorted or that have down strokes pushing either to the right or to the left. Such lower loops indicate a psychological effect of past unpleasant experiences in relationships, or what you felt to be an "un-normal" physical expression. This may be due to actual experience which was traumatizing, or it may be due to an attitude that developed regarding confusing involvement in one or more relationships.

These types of lower loops can also indicate the effect we have experienced regarding what we believed were parental requirements in relationships and attachments that were not totally comfortable.

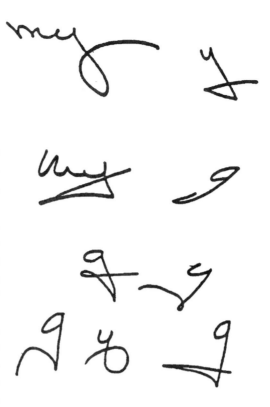

The effect of these past relationships remains. It is not necessary to discuss these discomforts specifically. The strengths you gain will allow you to deal with them satisfactorily. Discomfort in past relationships can also affect your present relationships.

DISCOMFORT REGARDING PRESENT RELATIONSHIPS:

Indicated by lower loops that are not completed, that is to say, that do not return to the baseline and cross the down stroke. (The effect of past relationships can be indicated simultaneously.)

Incomplete lower loops are evidence of frustration or discomfort in the material area in general and specifically in present people relationships. With these structures in your writing, you feel at a loss as to how to deal with them. You fear further discomfort and so avoid bringing them into your everyday reality where your mind and philosophy can handle them realistically. You may want to be alone, even if you like being sociable.

AGGRESSIVENESS:

Indicated by lower extenders that break away to the right below the baseline instead of looping to the left. The lower the break starts and the farther it thrusts to the right, the stronger the trait. This trait can also be seen in the letter *p*.

Aggressiveness is an act of resistance against an environment that you fear will prevent you from taking action toward your goal. It can cause you to push harder and move faster than is to your benefit. You try to shove your possibly imagined opposition out of the way before it can become an obstacle--an obstacle that may never arise. You may have a plan of action, but you are moving so aggressively that you can lose sight of it. This wastes energy and puts you psychologically off base. It can affect the sense of timing that allows you to operate according to schedule.

"...as a person making a show of his strength swims against the current of a river in flood and is soon drowned.".
....Kabir

MENTAL CONFUSION REGARDING ACTIVITY AND INTEREST:

Indicated as lower extenders and upper extenders strike against or intertwine with those above or below them. The mind is in confusion.

"What should I do first?" "What should I think about first?" The mind is being required to deal with so many thoughts and activities that it cannot compartmentalize and handle them systematically in an appropriate and comfortable manner. This is less likely to happen if upper and lower extenders are in proportion. You are then more apt to allow enough space between your lines.

Practice Assignment:

Form many of these upper and lower loops separately. Then practice them in combinations of upper and lower loops: *gh, yh, kg, ky, bg, yb,* etc.

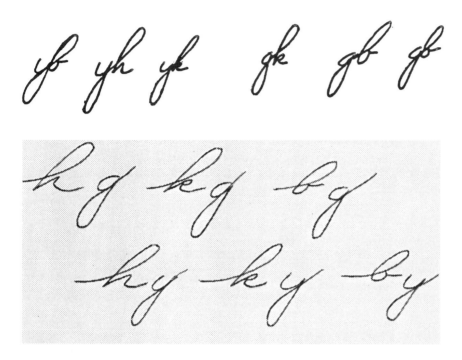

Use the letters and combinations of letters in words and phrases:

The bough is breaking
The gong is ringing

The boy is young
The girl is coughing

Please give rein to your ingenuity in finding ways to use these balance strokes. Practice them until they feel natural, at least twenty minutes a day, and any time the mind doesn't need to be fully occupied, such as when on the telephone or watching

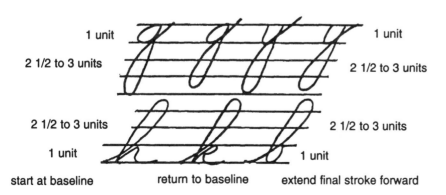

start at baseline   return to baseline   extend final stroke forward

television, etc. Doodlers can make good use of doodling. The more you practice, the faster it happens and the sooner you experience your intelligence and joy coursing through your being. In fact, it begins immediately.

As you form these strokes proportionately, as described, you experience in yourself an awareness of greater freedom and relaxation. You are developing your own inner reality. This is essential if you want to deal satisfactorily with your outer reality.

Practice Page

Please change only the structures you have already studied.
Do not attempt or force any other alterations.

h
g
k
y
b
f
m
n
n
a
d
o
g
s
i
t

a
b
c
d
e
f
g
h
i
k
m
n
o
r
s
t
y
z
s

AN UNFORGETTABLE YOUNG MAN

His mother brought him, a tall, bulky 15 year old, for graphotherapy hoping it could help him pass from Junior High School into High School. He had been in remedial classes throughout his school days.

At our first session he plopped his large body down solidly onto the chair, seeming to want to give the impression of being inanimate, except for his determination to wait out the allotted time without a hint of recognizing there was another person at the table beside him.

When he was convinced that I understood him and the reasons behind his so-called failures he became a part of the event. His underdeveloped writing showed incorrect spelling, reversed letters; his learning capabilities were clogged by mental repression of emotional hurts along with other limiting factors. He said he couldn't read and indeed he couldn't, surely not well enough to study his lessons in school.

He left, having practiced the suggested changes in his writing. During the week that followed I spoke with his mother who said he had not been doing his writing. He came back at the end of the week for a second session. He confessed that he had practiced at school, out of sight of his parents. It was a glorious ending to this visit, when he threw his arms high in the air and exclaimed, "I can read, I can spell, I can read, I can spell!" The vitality in that young man was a sight to behold.

Circumstances prevented his coming for more graphotherapy sessions. He did, however, graduate from High School and has established a business of his own. A remarkable and memorable person.

CHAPTER FOUR
The Capacity to Organize

Organizational ability requires perfect balance between the abstract and material zones.

When you have organizational ability you are able to imagine a concept, and simultaneously imagine the material manifestation of the concept. The ability to organize has to do solely with abstract penetration and imagination and material penetration and imagination. There is no thought process involved.

While organizational ability is an important asset to your thinking, thinking is not a part of the organizational process.

The capacity to organize is revealed in the letter *f*.

As you can see, the mental area is not a part of this structure. After you have imagined the concept and its manifestation, or the final product, the mind goes to work to plan and complete the project. If the abstract and material images are unclear the mind cannot cut out a clear path for itself. This trait does not necessarily reflect overall balance in the personality structure. Writing may show overall disproportion among the three areas and at the same time reveal organizational ability, or vice versa.

For your organizational ability to serve you correctly, to carry you toward your goals, you need first to develop your tri-dimensional balance as you did in Chapter Three.

ORGANIZATIONAL ABILITY:
Indicated by the upper and lower extenders of the letter f being of the same length and width, the width being in near proportion to that of your other upper and lower loops.

The first stroke of the letter must begin at the baseline, as in all abstract loops. The stroke must reach up into the abstract zone to form a smooth, well proportioned loop as it returns down to and extends below your baseline to its proportionate lower length. You then move back up toward the baseline forming and completing the lower loop as the up stroke connects with the down stroke, or "backbone" of the structure. It can also form an additional loop, or tie, as it reverses direction, coming back toward the right.

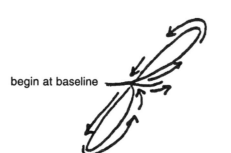

begin at baseline

(The "tie" is not a qualification for this trait).

Your final stroke must move forward to the right to complete the organizational process, and your mind moves toward its work.

If your *f* is unbalanced you can see for yourself whether your difficulty is in conceptualizing or in materializing or in both. You must imagine both the abstract and concrete aspects equally to be a successful organizer.

My Personal Handwriting

Practice Assignment:

Practice many proportional *f* structures. As you are able to execute this formation you will sense an inner rhythmic flow to enhance the effect of the well-proportioned upper and lower loops of the structures which contain the mental area, the middle zone:

gh, yh, bg, by, kg, ky

As you did earlier, use combinations of these letters in words, phrases and sentences, taking note that you are forming them in proper proportion.

fluff huff gaffer fibber folk ferry farthing fury finger fake faith fathom fuming

You are self-graphotherapists. You can evaluate for yourself the accuracy of your formation.

During daily frustrations, if you practice the organizational structure along with the balance strokes already learned, you can feel your sense of self returning. As you continue to practice, difficult happenings will elicit less frustration.

Practice Page

Please change only the structures you have already studied.
Do not attempt or force any other alterations.

h
g
k
y
b
f
m
n
n
a
d
o
g
s
i
t

a
b
c
d
e
f
g
h
i
k
m
n
o
r
s
t
y
g
s

"Selfishness is the greatest curse of the human race."
William Ewart Gladstone

"Sweet mercy is nobility's true badge."
William Shakespeare

"The very great is very small . . . and he has all who gives his all."
Michail Naimy

"Let greed be ever less in thee, and more content possess thee still."
Omar Khayyam

"A miser is as much in want of what he has as of what he has not."
Publilius Syrus

"Not he who has little, but he who wishes more is poor."
                    Seneca

*"Let us open up our natures, throw wide the doors of our hearts and
let in the sunshine of good will and kindness."*
                    O.S. Marsden

"The only gift is a portion of thyself."
                    Ralph Waldo Emerson

*"Kindness in words creates confidence,
Kindness in thinking creates profoundness,
Kindness in giving creates love."*
                    Lao-tze (604? - 531 B.C.)

CHAPTER FIVE
Generosity

*G*enerosity has been the counsel of prophets, poets and saints of all time. All great teachers of universal truth have given the same instruction.

She is a generous person

He is also generous

Long endings on words indicate the trait of generosity.

With your inner consciousness to direct it, generosity--the quality of true generosity--becomes one of the strongest indications of fearlessness.

Generosity enhances your thinking. Your mind is willing to give and receive. Your mind can move forward freely from thought to thought, from action to action.

Generosity has no self-serving purpose. If one exists it is because of psychological impediments that affect intelligent functioning. There is no thought of reciprocation. It gives solely to benefit the receiver. You feel joy, not as a consequence of having given but because of the freedom, the lack of fear, that had permitted your giving.

GENEROSITY can be seen when words end in final strokes that are at least as long as the width, but not more than two-and-one-half times as long as the width of the final letter of the word.

It is a slightly upward-curving stroke resembling an extended palm.

The trait is strengthened when the energy of the stroke, or the pressure you exert on the paper as you write, remains constant to the end of the stroke without feathering or fading out, and without growing heavier or becoming blunt.

Webster defines generosity as "liberality in spirit or act...fullness of spirit or strength." Generosity comes from the Latin meaning noble, or well-born.

Observe your personal writing and the samples of other "real" handwriting found heretofore, in the Appendix, and elsewhere.

Generosity of love and thoughts, of material substance, generosity in sharing anything that we feel would be of value to the receiver, is an indication of maturity, of faith, of courage. This maturity has nothing to do with chronological age; Webster defines maturity as "relating to a condition of full development." Children can sometimes evidence more maturity than adults.

The final stroke

moves forward

toward the

next word

final stroke moves

forward toward

the right

is a sample of

Lady Bird Johnson

Lady Bird Johnson

Lack of a true spirit of generosity is based on fear, fear of not having enough, of not being appreciated, of losing something we want...we can identify our own reasons. Our fears can manifest in selfishness, even stinginess.

> Idealistic as the trait of generosity may seem, it is of practical value in everything you do.

Generosity frees the thinking. The mind gives and receives without the burden of fear; exchange of ideas comes easily. Acts of courtesy are spontaneous and independent of learned behavior.

Energy flows forward, rhythmically, to the next thought, without being wasted in halted, backward or other extraneous movements that can reverse the direction of your energy.

Generosity does not boost your ego. It is not based on emotional attachment only, nor extended for your own sentimental satisfaction.

My Personal Handwriting
Write about any fears or phobias you might have.

Generosity is a quality of an integrated, fearless, joyful person. As a true giver, you may forget that you have given.

Some, however, even when experiencing this spontaneous generosity, can be struck with a sudden twinge of one or more of the following fears, fears that can halt your generosity dead in it tracks.

THE STROKE OF GENEROSITY CAN ELIMINATE THE FOLLOWING FEARS:

- INDECISIVENESS: Fear of the finality of a decision.

- BLUNTNESS: Fear of changing your mind.

- DESIRE FOR ATTENTION: Fear of not being appreciated

- SELF-CASTIGATION: Fear of being unworthy of the attention you crave.

- DISCONSOLATION: Fear of being incapable of handling daily circumstances.

- TENACITY: Fear of letting go.

- EXTRAVAGANCE: Fear of not giving and receiving enough.

When you regain your innate generosity, supported by your inner consciousness, these fears, or combinations of fears, automatically disappear.

As you practice the strokes representing your generosity these uncomfortable traits flee. They cannot exist in the presence of your freedom from fear. Your inner sense of balance and integrity which you have already achieved tells you where and how to direct your giving.

INDECISIVENESS:

Indicated by word endings that feather out or fade away. The weaker the final stroke, the more pronounced the trait.

Indecisiveness is the fear of the finality of a decision, of making an irrevocable mistake.

This fear threatens your generosity. You can change your mind about giving, not because you have rationally decided that your gift is inappropriate but because you are afraid that, for one reason or another, it might be, and that the consequences will last forever.

Indecisiveness can haunt people of all ages, professions, personal situations, and degree of success.

Indecisiveness reduces your mental effectiveness.

It causes the mind to vacillate without logical reason: "Should I, or should I not?"

Some find difficulty only in making major decisions; some can't decide what color tooth brush to buy!

Some vacillate only in making personal decisions, others only in professional ones. For some, any decision is a pain!

Pressure is energy. When the final stroke fades away, diminishes in strength or depth, energy diminishes. Frustration with the decision-making process sets in.

The mind gets bored and wants to change the subject.

It escapes making a final decision by going from one to another.

Without this fear you can still weigh the pros and cons logically and can change your mind if that is what is needed. But you do so from choice rather than fear.

When this is the case, you can decide without the element of fear. Your final strokes will end with the same pressure with which they began. They do not feather or fade away.

Nor do they end bluntly:

BLUNTNESS:

Indicated by final strokes that grow heavier as they end. They may even end in a ball-like period.

With this blunt ending you are afraid to alter your decision and so eliminate the possibility of beneficial change.

This trait manifests an over-exertion of energy, an over-decisiveness that prevents a rational changing of your mind. The flow of energy stops, is plugged up; it cannot flow forward evenly and freely.

DESIRE FOR ATTENTION:

Indicated by final strokes that rise to extend higher than the middle zone. This is the fear of not being appreciated, of not receiving recognition, either as a person or for deeds performed.

If you feel that being loved is dependent upon what you share and do, the fear grows.

You may have extended yourself generously but have not been "thanked;" you may have felt rejected. A "thank you," a smile, any slight expression of real gratitude can be a sufficient reward.

The fear of not being appreciated becomes the need to receive attention.

The need for reciprocation, even if it only means a bit of attention, is opposed to your spirit of generosity, which prompted your desire to give.

Feelings of guilt begin to flutter and grow. When this happens, Desire for Attention takes on a partner called Self-Castigation.

SELF-CASTIGATION:

whip

is there

his her

it it is

back back

a little a

lot tot

made any

Indicated by final strokes that move upward, higher than the middle zone, as in Desire for Attention, then back to the left. The severity and longevity of your self-punishment is determined by the length of the whip, or backlash, and how frequently it occurs.

With this trait you are punishing yourself for whatever you may have done or believe you have done, or thought, to engender the guilt. You may actually be guilty, or you may be blaming yourself unjustly. Often those who are guilty can rationalize their action so there is no need for self punishment.

With the combination of Desire for Attention and Self-castigation, feelings are mixed. You want attention, but you feel you do not deserve it; you believe it is wrong to want this attention, and when it is given, you feel even more guilty and whip yourself more severely.

You pull back into yourself instead of reaching forward toward others and toward your goal.

You are expending a great deal of energy uselessly and destructively.

This self-castigating punishment, even though you feel it toward yourself, can sometimes be manifested belligerently toward others.

DISCONSOLATION:

Indicated when the baseline of letters, often the final letter of a word, moves suddenly downward. The strength of this trait depends upon the frequency of the stroke and how far down it droops.

This is representative of the feeling that something, or many things, are going wrong and that you are helpless to do anything about it.

When the trait is attached to the strokes coming up from the lower, material zone, your disconsolation is sometimes accompanied by a concern relating to finances.

This kind of depression can develop to the point of feeling destructive toward self.

With the trait of generosity the final stroke is carried forward, with a slight upward curve; it cannot drop down and still be generosity. In the case of strokes coming from the lower zone, they move on upward and forward; the stroke never descends. Generosity displaces fear. Depression turns to optimism. Intelligent perspective is renewed.

TENACITY:

Indicated by final strokes that end in leftward-turning hooks.

This hook often occurs without the length required by the generosity stroke. But, even with the generous length, the hook reverses the flow of energy and of generosity.

The tenacity hook is found most frequently at the end of a word and in a t-bar. It can be seen elsewhere and in any zone.

With this final hook, the extended hand of generosity curls back to cling to what you had intended to give. It is hanging on to what you have acquired.

When you are functioning intelligently, maturely, this trait is a burden; it's a waste of energy.

Tenacity causes us to cling to something, property, people or ideas, when it would be more productive to release them. Tenacity limits one of our most constructive assets, generosity.

EXTRAVAGANT GENEROSITY:

Indicated by final word endings that are overly-long.

If these strokes extend longer than 2 1/2 times the width of the preceding letter, generosity becomes a protection against an environment that you feel might attack you if you do not treat it with extreme generosity.

At the same time, by creating a wider space between words, this overly-long stroke puts excessive psychological distance between you and your environment, keeping it at arm's length. You are afraid you cannot relate or deal with it if you allow it to live next door.

defense
share
all
give
as
more

When the actual space between words, with or without the final long stroke, extends more than 2 1/2 times the width of the final letter of the word, you can find yourself feeling more generosity toward yourself than toward others.

much   space
between   words
distance   from
others   luxury
for   us
elbow   room

If you have this trait:

• You want luxury for yourself, be it in time, elbow-room or things.

• You feel you need more than you have in order to survive in an oppressive atmosphere.

•You can feel your environment will absorb even the air you breathe if you do not keep it away. "Come see me, but don't stay too long."

•You can be interested in people while at the same time you are afraid "they" will crowd in on you, encroach upon your "ten acres," your space. Your fear may or may not be justified. Either way, your good judgment, your preferred choice can replace your fear.

In cultivating generosity, you are cultivating a most essential component of an integrated, fearless, joyful person.

Practice Assignment:

Practice word endings as prescribed:

The length equal to one-to-two-times the width of the preceding letter; a softly curving stroke that does not rise higher than the structure to which it is attached; endings that are not feathered or blunt; pressure, energy, that is consistent; absence of any hook.

Care news be for

pen word cheer

Create words, phrases, sentences that include all of the formations practiced heretofore, using individual originality and imagination. Look at other writings that are shown on sample pages and also those that come your way in your personal or business life.

Practice Page

Please change only the structures you have already studied.
Do not attempt or force any other alterations.

h
g
k
y
b
f
m
n
n
a
d
o
g
s
i
t

a
b
c
d
e
f
g
h
i
k
m
n
o
r
s
t
y
z
s

Calvin Coolidge

"No legacy is so rich as honesty."
William Shakespeare

"Such is the irresistible nature of truth, that all it asks, and all it wants, is the liberty of appearing."
Thomas Paine

"Can there be a more horrible object in existence than an eloquent man not speaking the truth?"
Carlyle

"Truth is the highest thing a man can keep."
Chaucer

"A lie can travel half way around the world while the truth is putting on its shoes."
Mark Twain

"There is no greater lie than a truth misunderstood."
William James

"We lie loudest when we lie to ourselves."
Eric Hoffer

CHAPTER SIX
Sincerity (Relating honestly and accurately in communications with others and self.)

When you relate with others honestly and sincerely, your words and actions come from the wealth of your inner being, your own sense of integrity, and not from a need for any kind of personal gain. You are free to speak and act from intelligent choice as opposed to the psychological fear of not achieving some kind of selfish purpose if you are honest.

Manners of communicating with others and with yourself are found in the formation of your "circle" letters, *a* and *o* and in the "circle" parts of the letters *d* and *g*.

a a a o o o d
d d o d d a d
g g g g a o d

good word make
dandelion on
gold gold an an
on on an did

My Personal Handwriting

Write about a situation when you were feeling uncomfortable.

When you are honest with others you are also honest with yourself. You do not deceive or manipulate your own mind in order to select words and actions that will give the impression of forthrightness. You need not maneuver it to your advantage or to others' disadvantage. It is fear that causes us to be dishonest, to lie, to steal, to evade, to connive, to win personal points. When you deceive others you deceive yourself. You convince yourself, for the moment at least, that what you are saying is true; or that you are justified in being out-and-out deceptive. You look for excuses and then look for the means to make your dishonesty both effective and palatable.

SINCERE COMMUNICATION:

Indicated by "circles" that are clear, un-contaminated, free of extraneous loops, lines, and hooks. The circles may be either open or closed at the top. This trait denotes your intent to be honest. You are not afraid of the truth, and do not feel compelled to alter it. Having achieved stable, well balanced maturity, you can be discriminating in what you say and also relate honestly and kindly.

When you have no selfish purpose, when you have no need to escape reality, you have no need to disguise the truth, to mislead either yourself or others.

The primary factor in sincere communication is motivation.

When your intent is pure, when you are in no way wanting gain of any kind for yourself, you can make a statement that is false, solely for another's benefit, and your handwriting will not show any manner of deception. Once, however, your mind becomes fearful of the result to your own personal self, your handwriting changes and reveals the manner in which you have moved from sincerity to insincerity.

You may tell yourself you do not want to hurt someone's feelings, but if any lack of sincerity is exhibited in your handwriting, you can look for your additional motive.

The mind cannot function clearly as long as it employs any form of deception. If you deceive yourself and others it is because you are afraid to deal with people, circumstances, and yourself, realistically.

When you clear the mind of the entanglement of deceit you open it to that spark of intuition, your sixth sense, that alerts the mind, enhances your thought processes, and adds originality to your thinking, your creativity and inventiveness.

Now that you have restored your inner balance, your inner

consciousness, your sense of integrity, the source of your real strength, you can alter your communication strokes with comfort and confidence. The truth will flow forth naturally and benevolently.

The following structures represent traits that waste time, intelligence and energy. They interfere with your rational thinking and sometimes nullify it. They can become compulsive habits of communicating, and they often close the door to your intuition. They contribute to personal pressure and threaten your relationships with others and yourself.

When writing is small and tight these strokes may be difficult to discern.

SELF DECEIT:

Indicated by a loop inside the left side of the "circle."

You are eliminating information from yourself. You are psychologically escaping facts that you know exist. If you do not want to acknowledge information, or an intuitive hint that has clearly presented itself, you dismiss it from your consciousness, deceiving yourself into believing it is not there. Self-deception can be passed along; you can relate a falsehood without consciously realizing it. You are irrationally escaping the truth. This trait has foreclosed the achievement of many major goals and has caused rifts in relationships. Under its influence, smart, rational thinking ceases to be rational because the mind has been denied access to accurate information.

SECRETIVENESS:

Indicated by a loop inside the right side of the "circle."

This trait denotes a psychological fear of, and protection against, revealing your personal, private self, your feelings, thoughts and activities. This fear causes you to withdraw. It is a pulling back within, that reverses the flow of energy. It can cause compulsive, protective outer behavior. It has caused some persons to move literally to another area, even to another continent, to avoid revealing themselves. Even so, the fear remains. Physical escape cannot eliminate the fear and compulsion for self-protection. Here again, it is not a rational decision to reveal or not to reveal, but a psychological fear of the outcome if you should allow yourself to confide whatever it is that you feel compelled to hide.

INTENTIONAL DECEIT:

Indicated by loops inside both sides of the "circle."

If you see this formation in your handwriting you are intentionally deceiving others either with or without the desire to do harm. This conscious deception can be used for your own emotional self-protection or it can be to take advantage of others. Whether it is malicious or not, it comes from fear that jeopardizes your inner peace. It burdens your mind and relationships. It promotes unsocial behavior. It is not an intelligent response to reality. You can use it either as a weapon or an unnecessary shield. You are acting from compulsion instead of from intelligent choice.

EVASIVENESS:

Indicated by a variety of formations within, and sometimes outside the "circle." It occurs also in the letter c, a half circle.

With this trait, you are evading the truth. Here again, you may do this with or without intent to harm, but it is always with intent to gain. Evasiveness is caused by fear of not being understood as you would wish. You may not be lying, but you are not truthful. You are "beating around the bush" to achieve a desired result. This trait contains a built-in loop-hole in case you are challenged.

The need to evade can be as simple as not wanting to hurt someone's feelings, but there is always the element of fear that, if nothing more, you may lose respect, credit or good will if the truth be told. It can also be used malevolently to do much harm. With this trait you tangle your thought processes until the mind doesn't know what it thinks. You can be misunderstood because you have twisted both your thoughts and your words. You can defeat your purpose and, when discovered, bring discredit to yourself. This is the need to benefit yourself regardless of how another is affected.

Within the trait of evasiveness three other traits, acquisitiveness, resentment, and self-deceit, can be found. These traits can appear either singly or in combination. Acquisitiveness and resentment will be discussed further in a later chapter.

ACQUISITIVENESS:

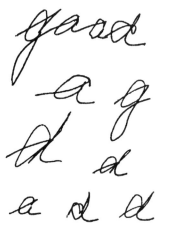

This can be seen when there is a hook within or beyond the "circle." The hook tells us that you are trying to grasp, through the manner in which you communicate, your own end result. You cannot be open. You do not trust your intelligence to lead you toward the best for all, including yourself. You do not speak from choice but from the fear of not acquiring.

RESENTMENT:

Represented by the initial straight, rigid stroke, starting at or below the baseline, it indicates a fear of imposition. "If I don't manipulate them, they will do it to me" Your intelligence is not working for you.

SELF-DECEIT:

You have become acquainted with this trait. It is the cutout area inside the left side of the circle. Here, however, being accompanied by resentment and acquisitiveness, the "loop" is misshapen.

To come across persuasively and/or to satisfy the wish to be, or appear to be, sincere, you resort to self-deceit, convincing yourself that what you are saying is true. Consequently you are understood "wrong," and, being misunderstood, you can be surprised, or feign surprise, depending upon your original motivation.

If your handwriting shows any of these formations you are evading the truth; you are misdirecting it in a conniving manner, because you are afraid of revealing your true motive.

With these manners of communication your mind may be operating craftily, but not intelligently.

It should be particularly noted that any lack of sincerity in your communications reduces clear mental functioning. Even your most logical thought process cannot achieve accurate conclusions if the mind is programmed with misinformation. When you clear your mind of the stress of fear you can perceive and communicate accurately. Your mind is released to accept your spark of intuition that is valuable at all times, under any circumstance.

Having secured your integrated, balanced self and your spirit of generosity, you can look at your "circle" formations and recognize how you are communicating. Now that you have instilled firmly within yourself your source of true inner strength, you can forego the escapes and resistances that have inhibited your ability to communicate and behave forthrightly. You can adjust your handwriting to reveal open sincerity. If you will compare your first sample of writing with your present writing, you may find that these structures have already made constructive changes.

Practice Assignment:

Practice clear, uncontaminated circle formations, It is very helpful in forming these strokes to eliminate all approach, or lead-in strokes. Start the circle at the top of the letter, thus diminishing the possibility of contamination. This is indicative of the trait of directness, which will be discussed in Chapter Eleven; it allows the mind to formulate and communicate subject matter, directly to the point.

With approach strokes:

Without approach strokes:

Combine these circle formations with structures already conquered in Chapters three, four and five. For instance:

fog gaff hod day dog hag caddie hag
gag yak fad hay gay boy bog bag of
off cog coy agog gag hack do chock
cockade add had do cod zoo bad baggy

Practice Page

Please change only the structures you have already studied.
Do not attempt or force any other alterations.

h
g
k
y
b
f
m
n
n
a
d
g
s
i
t

a
b
c
d
e
f
g
h
i
k
m
n
o
r
s
t
y
z
s

Walt Disney

"The burden of life is lighter when I laugh at myself."
  Tagore

"You grow up the day you have the first real laugh...at yourself."
  Ethel Barrymore

"I have a fine sense of the ridiculous, but no sense of humor."
  Edward Albee

CHAPTER SEVEN
Your Sense of Humor

Humor can be wry, witty, sarcastic. There are punsters, comics, pranksters, clowns, kidders-on-the-square. If you have a true sense of humor you laugh, irresistibly, at yourself. You can keep yourself and your situations in perspective.

Maude   Man   Mom

Nancy   Make   Hope

Even in the midst of this serious predicament called life, you do not take yourself too seriously. Throughout the ages, poets and philosophers have commended humor. It is commonplace that "laughter is the best medicine."

Most of us, no matter how intent we are upon maintaining propriety and handling every situation correctly, can make ridiculous mistakes. We can do and say things we wish we hadn't. We can be ignorant when we want to appear wise. We can behave nonsensically when we want to make sense. We can embarrass ourselves when we want to impress. Life can seem to be completely out of whack, and so can we.

My Personal Handwriting

Write about something you feel very good about

Theodore S. Geisel, better known as Dr. Seuss, says "humor has a tremendous place in a sordid world. It's more than just a matter of laughing. If you can see things out of whack, then you can see how things can be in whack."

Norman Cousins prescribed it for himself in his now famous recovery from "irreversible" illness.

THE SENSE OF HUMOR

stroke is usually found in the abstract area in certain capital letters, particularly *M* and *N*, but also in *U, V, Y, W,* and *H*. It can be added to the lower case forms of these letters. The humor stroke is that soft, curving, semi-circular-like flourish of the initial stroke. In capital letters it begins high, in the abstract area. In the middle area it reaches toward the abstract. If it were in an inverted position, it would have the curve of a smile. It is not rigid or angular but has a pleasing smoothness, the roundness of the top of a bubble, and this is the way you find yourself feeling, as if bubbles of laughter were breaking inside your breast. This does not mean that you are denied human sorrow. Your humor, along with your balance, generosity and sincerity, encourages your stream of inner joy to flow, helping you to see value in pain and grief. A true sense of humor can keep sadness from becoming despair.

Humor with a slightly different quality, one that shows the capacity to flirt with life and its unpredictables can be found in T-crossings that have a modest double curve.

Your sense of humor can rescue you, can bring you back to human reality. You can see yourself as actors playing a "real and earnest," but cheerful character who can also stumble and bumble through life's incongruities. You can look at your character objectively, with a sense of humor that doesn't require you to see yourself as being more competent, or less foolish, than others. You can laugh at your own foibles. This kind of humor helps you to be more understanding and sympathetic. It gives a light-hearted perspective which relieves the heaviness of life's burdens. Humor spikes life with zest.

Your sense of humor can help dissolve two traits that stem from psychological fear, the fear of not being loved: Jealousy, and the Need for Responsibility. These can be demanding, uncomfortable, and a waste of energy.

T-bars, double curve

JEALOUSY:

Is revealed in small inverted loops that attach themselves to the initial strokes in structures such as M, N, T, U, V, Y, W, and sometimes J. It can also be found in the lower case forms of these letters. To qualify, the loop must be on the left side of the initial stroke of the letter, and the loop must first move left and/or downward. The tighter the loop, the stronger the trait. Jealousy can also be found in the initial stroke of the personal pronoun, I. The shape of the loop can vary.

Fear of not being loved can be extremely painful, even injurious to both yourself and others. You feel that you must excel over others in everything that you attempt, because you believe that being the "best" is a prerequisite to being loved. This belief usually was conceived in childhood when you felt that being "best" was a parental requirement to winning love. You still feel that your worth as a person is dependent upon your impressive performance. Jealousy misdirects and misuses your energy.

DESIRE FOR RESPONSIBILITY:

This trait is indicated in much the same structure as the trait of jealousy. It is a loop that is in the same location and with similar shape, only larger. The loop has grown in size. Its shape can vary. The responsibility loop is often seen in the capital J and in the personal pronoun *I*, as well as in *M, N, T*, etc.

The trait of jealousy has been transmuted into exaggerated feelings of responsibility for others. It is an expansion from the solitary and lonely position and the fear of not being loved, to helping others by being responsible for them. The more responsible you are the more valuable you feel. This is your way of winning love, of acting out your fear, by taking care of others, as opposed to excelling over them. The fear remains, but is expressed differently.

You can be responsible without this trait, which can put inordinate pressure on you. With this trait you may tend to take responsibility that rightly belongs to others. You diffuse your energies, and may give the impression of not trusting others to be responsible. You can discourage their being responsible, even though that is not your intention.

You act from compulsion as opposed to rational choice. With a true sense of humor, along with all else you have accomplished, this need fades, and you are able to be more realistically responsible, without unnecessarily depleting your own resources that are required for your health and well being.

If you need responsibility to boost your feeling of self-worth, but are afraid of taking it, when you want it but wish that it were not required of you, the loop can flatten out on the bottom.

When the loop is not completed, when it does not touch the down stroke of the structure, you may not carry this responsibility through as you intended.

When the initial stroke of this large loop moves upward, without the immediate turn to the left, and meets the down stroke, the need for responsibility is revealed, but there is no fear of the task, and it will, if at all possible, be completed.

In the capital *J*, when the upper loop is in proportion with the lower loop and is not shaped as a "responsibility" loop, this trait is not indicated. Nor does it show in the personal pronoun *I*, when it is a single down stroke, when it is formed in "copy-book" fashion (as taught in school), or when it is printed.

Touches downstroke

Doesn't touch downstroke

Initial stroke moves upward

No need for responsibility

I am I run

I do I can

Practice Assignment:

m n H V W mamie

nancy merry muse n

m n H V W mamie

nancy merry muse

Practice the humor flourish until you feel that natural inner bubble of laughter. Use this stroke at every opportunity. Your sense of humor adds perspective to your more severe circumstances.

The "hook" is not required, but if it occurs naturally, it may be useful in maintaining humor.

J J J J

Practice the capital J until the upper and lower loops are in proportion and well formed. You may also use the printed J. If you do, the cross-bar must be evenly divided by the perpendicular stroke. A balanced *J*, and "copy book" form of the pronoun *I*, seem to be some of the more difficult structures to master.

Use whichever form of the personal pronoun "I" you like. However, it must not be taller than the loops of your *h, k,* and *b*. The cross-bars of the printed "*I*" must be the same length and evenly placed on the down stroke. The "copy-book" form must be uniform. This is a very personal structure. Included in its significance is your response to your parents. You will want to dismiss any non-constructive carry-over feelings. As you make this structure in the suggested manner you rid yourself of unresolved psychological reaction.

I bank I have

I I like

The single down stroke structure is simple and direct, and easily precludes psychological self-involvement. (Directness will be discussed more fully in a later chapter.)

The fear of not being loved by the person(s) from whom you most need love begins at a very young age and roots itself deeply within, motivating behavior in many ways. You can, however, dismiss this fear by changing your writing, thus freeing yourself to love, and to be loved, without these stressful psychological complications.

Humor is an important factor in dealing with this and all fears.

Practice Page

Please change only the structures you have already studied.
Do not attempt or force any other alterations.

h

g

k

y

b

f

m

n

n

a

d

o

g

s

i

t

a

b

c

d

e

f

g

h

i

k

m

n

o

r

s

t

y

z

s

"When I look back on all these worries I remember the story of the old man who said on his deathbed that he had a lot of trouble in his life, most of which never happened."
Winston Churchill

"If I knew what I was anxious about, I wouldn't be anxious."
Mignon McLaughlin

CHAPTER EIGHT
Logic Versus Repression and Worry

Individual minds operate in a variety of ways as they collect and process information and ideas. Regardless of content, your mind approaches subject matter in its own particular way. These various manners of thinking can be observed in the formations of the humps of the letters *m, n,* and *h.* You are not concerned with altering your thought processes as such. You do want to eliminate the strokes that are evidence of the irrational worry and mental repression that restrict the ability to think logically without unnecessary delay.

If you avoid emotional pains by mentally repressing them, storing them in an inaccessible closet, you bind your mind so tightly that your capacity to understand and critique quickly and accurately is relegated to a dormant state, unavailable for immediate use.

The fear of experiencing, or re-experiencing, heartaches thwarts the mind in its effort to access and assess information correctly.

Arriving at a logical conclusion can be a long and tedious process. The mind can continue to accumulate more and more information until it has enough to satisfy itself that there is no more. It may add 100 pieces to a 50-piece jig-saw puzzle.

When you mentally repress your emotional hurts you temporarily damage your conscious mental functioning.

A favorite hurt to conceal, to repress, is the feeling of guilt, which may, or may not, be justified.

If your writing shows this trait, you may be hiding justified guilt, not wanting to admit to yourself your intentional, unethical behavior.

My Personal Handwriting

What feelings are you hiding from yourself? What's worrying you right now?

You can also feel guilt over circumstances for which you are in no way responsible: your parents' incompatibility; your belief you are unworthy of being loved, respected; your belief that you have unintentionally hurt someone you wanted to please; or it can be as trivial as not being able to hurry as required of you.

Life-long migraine headaches have been known to disappear with the elimination of repression and worry.

REPRESSION:

Indicated by the retracing of the strokes between the humps of *m, n,* and the hump attached to *h* and *k.* It may also appear in other structures as shown in these illustrations.

The upstroke retraces the preceding downstroke. (The initial downstroke is retraced by the following upstroke.)

This can occur in *m* and *n,* and in *h* and *k* between the downstroke of the loop and the following upstroke.

It can also be found in certain *t* structures, in *v* and in certain forms of *r.*

To restate: A stroke moves down to the baseline. It retraces itself as it moves back up. This is repression. If a stroke moves upward first, then retraces itself as it moves downward, this is not repression.

When there is any degree of a v-shape between the strokes, the strength of the trait is lessened.

When the v-shape, or angle, reaches to the baseline the trait of repression is not present.

The consequences of repression accumulate. Pressures build under the mass of unacknowledged feelings. Headaches and abdominal un-ease can result. The mind can feel like exploding, particularly if the essential individual balance described in Chapter Three has not been achieved.

THE TRAIT CALLED WORRY:

The trait called worry enables us to fictionalize problems and situations that we expect to be impossible to handle in case they should occur. Worry is not rational concern about actualities. It is manufactured trouble.

Worry is seen in the same structures that show repression.

WORRY:

Indicated by inverted loops between the humps of the letters *m, n,* and in the letters *h, k, r, v, t.*

Worry, as understood here, is irrational. This is worry over imagined possibilities; it is not logical concern based on factual information.

Worry is the fear that the tide might not come in, or that the sky might fall, and that we are helpless to stop the catastrophe.

This fear makes it difficult to trust the judgment of others.If you have this fear, you contrive problems to justify your lack of trust.

With both repression and worry, our mind is, for the time being, clogged and not capable of intelligent reasoning.

When you forsake these traits you free yourself from your deeply closeted hurts, and you can see your past and present realistically. Your mind is able to assess circumstances rationally.

During this process you may re-experience your hurts, perhaps uncomfortably for the moment, because you are seeing them afresh. But you can take a logical point of view, see situations for what they are, as opposed to what you had believed they were, or would be if you allowed your mind to take a conscious look at them. You can now dismiss your unjustified guilt, and deal appropriately with what might be justified. The hurt fades into lesser importance.

We refer to the capacity of the mind to recognize and critique in this manner as the analytical thought process.

ANALYTICAL THINKING:

Indicated by V-shaped angles found most obviously between the humps of the letters m and n and in the h and k. As stated earlier, these angles can be found elsewhere, such as in t, r and v.

The V-shape found at the baseline of the letter can be used in letters that are either rounded at the top or angular at the top. It is the angular formation at the bottom of the letter that indicates the analytical thought process. The top of the structure is not relevant.

As you develop the analytical mental process, you automatically acquire the trait called initiative.

INITIATIVE:

Indicated by a stroke that breaks away and moves up from the downstroke after it has stopped at the baseline of a letter. It is usually found in *h*'s and *k*'s and in certain *t*-formations.

If you have this trait, you are not afraid to take the first step toward a goal. You can be a self-starter. Initiative is what the word implies: the ability to initiate action. You are not dependent upon someone to push you forward. It is not the desire to override or to be defensively aggressive; you are simply moving ahead without fearful hesitation.

There are two traits, found most obviously in your m and n, that no longer serve you well. Self-consciousness is a psychological fear. Superficial Thinking is an escape. Self-consciousness often accompanies Repression. Superficial Thinking is found in combination with a variety of other traits.

SELF-CONSCIOUSNESS:

Indicated by the graduating height of the humps of your *m* and *n*. Self-consciousness is the fear of ridicule and often accompanies repression. If you have this trait it is because you have felt ridiculed at some time, or perhaps frequently, and you anticipate that it will happen again. You are afraid you may look, speak, or behave in a manner that is inappropriate and unacceptable. Because of this fear, your mind pushes deeper, feeling compelled to gain more knowledge. You press yourself to learn more in order to feel more secure in situations and with people.

This has been a workable compensation in the past. Now, however, with your innate strength refreshed, you are free to learn as much as you want in any field of interest, but you do this from choice, rather than from the compulsion which has been prompted by fear. You can vanquish the pain of self-consciousness by not allowing any hump of your *m* or *n* to protrude higher than those preceding it.

SUPERFICIAL THINKING:

Indicated, as might be expected, in these "thinking" letters, m and n. Superficial thinking is evident when these letters are lower than the height of your other middle-zone structures. The mind is not penetrating deeply enough to probe and deal thoroughly with problems, or the work at hand. It is rebelling against thinking. You may have fine, alert thought processes, but you are leaving them in low gear, not putting them to best use. Your mind is being lazy. If the strokes of these letters are poorly formed, it indicates a deterioration in the actual thought process.

Some who have resorted to this escape trait try to get by on intuition alone. If you do this, you have convinced yourself that intuition can be a substitute for logical thought. It is thinking, however, that must carry through with the knowledge you have perceived through your intuition. Mental neglect reduces the effectiveness of your intuition.

Practice Assignment:

Practice opening up any retracing or loops until a wedge, angle, or v-shape is achieved at the baseline of the strokes we have been describing as repression and worry. Do not be concerned with the tops of the humps. They may be round, pointed, or in any variation or combination of shapes. You are changing only the base of the structure where retracings and loops occur.

Worry

Repression

Worry and repression
are eliminated.

If your writing shows self-consciousness, do not allow succeeding humps of your *m* and *n* to rise above the previous humps.

Self-conscious

Self-consciousness
eliminated

If your writing shows superficial thinking, you can bring your mind back into dependable, realistic functioning by raising the strokes of your m and n to the height of surrounding middle-zone structures.

hammer hammer

Superficial thinking

minor mental

---

hammer hammer

Probing
mental activity

more mental

manner mental

Because you have learned to meet and deal with the every-day world, with people, situations and information, from the foundation of your personal sense of integrity, from the full and coordinated use of all of the aspects of your three-dimensional self, you no longer need to fear, or escape from, your best intelligent thinking.

With your resurrected integrated self, and with your clearer thinking you may recall past events more accurately and vividly, but without the prolonged acidic resentments, fierce guilts, and piercing longings for what cannot be.

Practice Page

Please change only the structures you have already studied.
Do not attempt or force any other alterations.

h
g
k
y
b
f
m
n
n
a
d
o
g
s
i
t

a
b
c
d
e
f
g
h
i
k
m
n
o
r
s
t
y
z
s

ABE LINCOLN

RICHARD NIXON

JOHN KENNEDY

"At a certain age some people's minds close up; they live on their intellectual fat."
William Lyon Phelps

CHAPTER NINE
Open Minded-ness

Broadmindedness, or open-mindedness, is a mental activity, not a philosophical concept. Your thinking broadens, or opens. Your mind is not afraid to observe and select from the potpourri that is presented to it. It can receive and consider ideas and information before accepting or rejecting it.

The closed, or narrow, mind tends to discard inputs automatically, either on the basis of prior bias or because it is fearful of dealing with whatever is being presented. The mind's door closes in resistance and escape. Of course, this fear restricts your free flow of energy.

OPEN-MINDEDNESS:

Readily discernible in the letter e, located in the middle-zone, the mental, mundane area.

When you open your mind, reasonably and without fear or resistance, the width of the structure is not less than one-half of, or wider than, the height of the loop. The broader the loop, the stronger the trait; the narrower the loop, the stronger the narrow-minded-ness. When the *e* contains no loop, the mind completely eliminates any input, for the moment at least, and sometimes forever, depending upon other traits. The mind moves in and out of information so rapidly, finding only what it wants to find, it can jump to the conclusion that what is there is not worth considering. If you are open-minded your mind is free to choose from the entire menu of ideas and information offered.

My Personal Handwriting

Write about when you'll listen and when you'll not listen to the ideas of others.

Now that you have secured your inner balance, generosity, sincerity, humor and logical thinking, you no longer need the escape of narrow-minded-ness; you need not restrict your choices.

"It is well to open one's mind but only as a preliminary to closing it. . . for the supreme act of judgment and selection."

. . . Irving Babbitt

On the other hand, when your loop is broader than its height, you have taken the door of your mind off its hinges and left yourself with no selectivity, no choice but to allow anything and everything to enter at will. Your mind has become non-discriminating, and you run the risk of subjecting yourself to worthless and even harmful ideas and information.

"If you keep your mind sufficiently open, people will throw a lot of rubbish into it."

. . . William Orton

Practice Assignment:

Practice the structure of the letter *e*, separately and in words and groups of words, keeping the loops in proportionate height and width. Use ingenuity in devising sentences that will employ all of the characteristics you have been developing.

hear see select — Useful

very wide wide — Too broad

very closed close — Too narrow

Please change only the structures you have already studied.
Do not attempt or force any other alterations.

h
g
k
y
b
f
m
n
n
a
d
g
s
i
t

a
b
c
d
e
f
g
h
i
k
m
n
o
r
s
t
y
z
s

OLIVER WENDELL HOLMES, Jr.

"There is a paradox in pride; it makes some men ridiculous, but prevents others from becoming so."
Charles Caleb Colton

"Likeness begets love; yet proud men hate one another".
Thomas Fuller

Dadu: "False indeed are the conceit and vanity of this sheath of skin filled with air."

St. Luke: "For everyone that exalted himself shall be abased, and he that humbleth himself shall be exalted."

CHAPTER TEN
Independent Thinking and
Pride - True or False

hen you are truly independent in your thinking, you are not afraid to make decisions based on your logical, best judgment. You are not unduly influenced by others', possibly deprecating, opinions. You also are not afraid to consider their inputs.

With your open mind you can hear and consider outside suggestions thoroughly and then formulate and finalize decisions, independently.

You may want approval and admiration, and wish very much to please, but the fear of personal criticism or rejection does not threaten conclusions that are the outcome of your intelligent reasoning.

When accompanied by your previously acquired abstract, philosophical capacity, independent thinking helps your mind to focus on the issue or situation at hand and to put it into perspective, without the distraction of ego-involvement. Without fully developed abstract capacity, independent thinking can be detrimental.

INDEPENDENT THINKING:

Is found in the stems of the letters *d* and *t*. Using the circle area of the letter *d* as a unit of measure, if the stem of your *d* rises less than two units above the height of the circle area, or mid-zone of the letter, you are independent in your thinking regarding personal decisions and/or those that can reflect upon your personal worth. If the stem of your letter *t* rises less than double the

My Personal Handwriting

In growing up, what were the messages you received from your mother or father?

height of the middle-zone structures adjacent to it, you are independent in your thinking regarding your work or professional activities.

It is possible to be independent in your thinking about personal matters but not about your work or professional matters, and vice versa.

This is an appropriate point to speak of the philosophical loop of the letter *l*. This structure indicates independent thinking and pride regarding one's philosophy.

The loop of the letter *l* needs to be the same proportion as the stem of your independent *d* and *t*. If the loop stretches it means that you take an egotistical pride in your philosophical beliefs. As with all ego involvement, this can be distracting to your inner philosophical self and to your practical behavior.

It is essential to follow the suggested sequence of study. When you have developed your philosophical, abstract area, your balance and the other qualities found in earlier chapters, your independent thinking does not manifest itself as resistance to outside opinion. You are simply taking responsibility for forming your own final conclusions. But, without the indispensable proportionate support of your abstract, inner awareness, your independent thinking is no longer an asset. It serves you falsely. It can cause you to oppose a suggestion when it would be profitable to accept it. You are unable to see the subject matter as it relates to the whole, this being primary to accurate consideration and planning. If you have not secured your inner self, you may be independent in your thinking but you are dependent upon others to tell you what to believe--for your philosophical concepts, your code of ethics, your point of reference. Your capacity to conceptualize is limited. You negate the purpose of independent thinking. You are inclined to over-emphasize the immediate moment, situation or problem. It becomes huge because you are not seeing beyond it. This lack of perspective eliminates the constructive effect of independent thinking, making it difficult and often impossible to recognize a more advantageous point of view. You see the pinpoint and are oblivious to the surrounding area.

This trait, combined with Defiance of Authority, can cause you to lose out for no reason, except for your unreasonable resistance to any suggestion, regardless of the expertise of the counselor; you may find your face is minus its nose!

On the other hand, when you have accumulated the qualities previously presented, independent thinking is a fine and valuable trait, one that is to be desired.

You can also lose your independent thinking if you acquire a false sense of pride, when your desire for others to hold you in high regard overrides your intelligent and realistic observation of yourself, your opinions and your work.

You may, or may not, give the impression of being independent in your thinking. Nevertheless your fear of being imperfect in the eyes of others as well as of yourself, can cause you to be dependent upon outside opinions and to use the conclusions of another even if they are invalid. You can lose track of what you, yourself, feel and think.

This fear originated in your younger years when you felt you disappointed, or didn't live up to the expectations of, someone of utmost importance to you, and that your perfection, alone, could win the coveted respect of that person. Or, in some instances, you may have come to believe that you were regarded highly because you were given the impression that you were perfect in that person's eyes, and that if you do not remain so you will lose love and respect. Your value came to be dependent upon the value another assigned to you.

Faced with ego-extinction, you needed to pretend, even to yourself, at times, that you believed you were indeed perfect; all the while your feeling of inadequacy churned beneath the disguise.

The fear of being imperfect can cause you to escape into a boot-strapping pseudo-self-confidence. Simultaneously you are beset by the devastating fear of failure if you should set goals in accord with your true talents and desires. You can crush achievable dreams before you have given them warranted consideration.

FALSE SENSE OF PRIDE:

As the stem of the letter d rises to more than twice the height of the circle-area, you are taking on the psychological protectiveness of a false sense of personal pride, basing your worth as a person on others' evaluations. The stem of the d may be either retraced or looped.

If the stem of the letter *t* is more than twice the height of the adjacent mid-zone structures, you have adorned yourself with a false sense of pride about your work and activities. The taller the stems in proportion to the middle-zone structure, the stronger the trait. The stem may be either retraced or looped.

Here again, your philosophical/abstract ability and balance is absolutely vital. If you bootstrap your self-confidence so high, and do not consider the unknown, abstract aspect of achievement that allows you to plan concretely toward your goal, you can lose track of practical reality. If your elevated feeling of pride remains, and you have lost the support of your abstract inner consciousness, you can be so elated with what you now know is your capacity to attain high, long-range and/or dream goals, you can lose sight of the practical necessity of getting the job planned, started and completed. You can stay on your newly-found Cloud Nine. Your false sense of pride, your pretended independent thinking, can seem real to you. Your excitement may say, "I can do that! Of course, I can do that; in fact, I've already done it!"

Consequently, you can neglect to begin a project because you see it as already accomplished. Thus, you can repeat your disappointment in yourself, and "believe" you have validated the disappointment of another, while at the same time giving an opposite impression.

You can come across as a "know-it-all," "I'm great stuff," pretending you are self confident while at the same time you feel inferior, and under-estimate your ability to achieve. You can limit yourself to un-challenging goals, inasmuch as any thought of possible failure is devastating. Your highest desires can be crushed before you've given yourself a chance to consider them.

In the many hundreds of examples I have studied, this trait harks back to your relationship with your father and what you believed his expectations of you to be. It can be associated with the choosing of a profession; a versatile youth, because of diverse talents, finds it difficult to make a specific choice and hears, or thinks he hears, "Son, you're 16 (more or less), it's time for you to decide what you're going to do with your life". The most brilliant mind can feel frozen under such pressure. The young person may think, "If I follow in my father's footsteps he'll respect me;" "I must choose a profession that's prestigious or will be highly paid;" "I have to decide on something right now;" "I must succeed at whatever I do." Or it is possible that a sibling, or even a friend, may be given more credit and attention than you feel you have received or deserved. This trait can stem from a father's absence, or by his death, even if the child has never known, or does not remember the father. In women it can also be attributed to the idea, "He's proud of me now, I must never fail him;" or it may be a combination of associations. This excessive pride or vanity occurs more frequently in men than in women.

Practice Assignment:

Form many *d*'s and *t*'s with stems in proper proportion with the middle-zone structures. Incorporate them into words that also contain all you have learned. Abstract loops must always be higher than the stems of *d* and *t*. Use *d* and *t* in words and sentences until they feel comfortable.

daughter throng healthy youth

dandy doth dough threading

shouting shedding fiftieth dish

dearth earthy basting banding

bathing smoothly bending both

Practice Page

Please change only the structures you have already studied.
Do not attempt or force any other alterations.

h
g
k
y
b
f
m
n
n
a
d
o
g
s
i
t

a
b
c
d
e
f
g
h
i
k
m
n
o
r
s
t
y
z
s

CHAPTER ELEVEN
Directness

The trait of directness helps to focus your thinking, to lead your mind to the crux. It assists in cutting through extraneous material and thoughts to get to the heart of the subject. While it is not necessary to psychological health, it can play a part in ridding you of other unsatisfactory characteristics. This trait can be pertinent in any vocation or circumstance, and as you found in Chapter Six, it enhances your ability to communicate clearly. You can be direct in your thinking and communicating and also be diplomatic and sensitive in expressing your thoughts.

When the mind functions with the added efficiency provided by combining this trait with those already acquired, there is little opportunity to indulge in certain psychological fears and resistances, to which we shall also attend in this chapter.

This trait is a consistent and satisfactory asset only when you have achieved the characteristics found in earlier chapters.

DIRECTNESS:

Indicated when the approach stroke found in many structures is eliminated. There is no stroke leading into the letter. The initial stroke starts at the top of the letter and comes down to the baseline. The stroke may be straight or curved, as required by the formation of the structure.

My Personal Handwriting

Write about a relationship in which you would like to improve communications.

With this trait your mind approaches problem-solving, decision-making, performance and communications by going directly to the core, eliminating non-essential information or ideas.

In the letters *t, i, m, n, u, v, w,* as well as in the circle letters, *a, o, d, g,* omit the up-stroke that starts at the baseline. Begin the letter at the top of the first down stroke. In some of these letters you have the opportunity to use the humor flourish, always a welcome addition. Humor does not distract from directness and can add to the practicality of dealing with weighty, day-to-day activities. This simple, unadorned stroke can also be used in capitals.

NOTE: Remember that the trait of directness is a detriment in the abstract structures, *h, k, b* and *f.* The abstract is not a mental process; the mental is not abstract; the term directness, as used here, applies to a mind-activating trait. You are already using the correct formation of the abstract strokes.

The trait of directness helps you to forsake more easily the discomforts of: stubbornness, resentment, sensitivity to criticism, anger, and argumentativeness. Mental directness snips off the opportunity to become involved with such psychological impediments. You may have needed them for survival tools at some time in the past. Now, with all your inner strength constantly available, these resistances are like tin soldiers confronting an illusionary enemy. Logical reasoning and psychological resistance are at odds with each other.

STUBBORNNESS:

ten tan

is in

ten tan

is in

d d

d d

d d

Indicated in t-stems and d-stems that are braced, tent-like. This bracing may also be found elsewhere, as in *i*. The more pronounced the bracing and the more frequently it appears, the stronger the trait. Using directness in the *t* and *i* precludes the appearance of the trait.

Stubbornness in your *t* means you are psychologically, not logically, resisting real, or imagined interference regarding your work activities.

In your *d*, the resistance regards personal matters. The trait of directness in d applies only to the circle area, not the stem. Bracing cannot occur when you retrace your d-stem down to the baseline.

This trait reflects the attitude, "Right or wrong, I'm right." You plant your feet in a firmly, braced stance to resist anything or anyone who, you feel, is intruding upon your decision-making, your independence, or is depriving you of your "deserved rights." Even though you may have had good reason for resorting to stubbornness, when it takes over, thorough reasoning can diminish or vanish altogether.

RESENTMENT:

d

s to to

to w

p is

d p

s p

to to

p u

p is

Indicated when the initial up stroke of a structure is straight and rigid. It starts at or below the baseline. It must be straight. If the stroke curves it is not resentment. The longer the stroke, the farther below the baseline it starts, the stronger the resistance. And, as in all traits, the frequency of occurrence strengthens its hold on you.

Resentment is a resistance against imposition. It results from having been, or having felt you have been, imposed upon, personally and/or professionally.

You recall that the *t* refers to your work or activity, and the *d* to yourself personally. You may have had to resist your propensity for saying "yes" when "no" would have been wiser. Your generosity may not have been appreciated. You may have felt unjustly criticized. This trait can be painful and destructive. It always misuses energy.

SENSITIVITY TO CRITICISM: (Fear of Disapproval)

Indicated by loops in the *d*-stem and the *t*-stem. The wider the loop, the greater the fear, and the anticipation of disapproval.

A very broad loop indicates that you feel guilty because you believe you deserved to be criticized, even though it may have been unfounded. This loop, regardless of size, tells you that, in some way, you feel that criticism has been deserved, that you have always been criticized and always will be, no matter how much you try to please. The loop may be found in *t*-stems and *d*-stems of any height, from very short to very tall.

This trait began in the past when you were hurt by criticism you felt coming from someone important to you, from whom approval was essential. Now you always expect criticism to be forthcoming.

When there is no loop, you are not afraid of criticism; you don't anticipate it. How you handle criticism may or may not be rational. You may resist it or you may see it for what it's worth. Your method of dealing with criticism will be constructive if you have achieved the traits you have been studying. You can see and act on criticism with good judgment, keeping others' observations in proper perspective. You have developed a sense of self-dignity and respect that can use valuable criticisms, and disregard others.

ANGER/TEMPER:

Indicated by very short, straight strokes preceding the initial stroke of a structure. These are called "temper tics." (As will be seen in a later chapter, temper is also found in another stroke.) The frequency with which this trait occurs indicates how constantly your anger persists.

When your writing shows temper tics, you are experiencing nagging feelings of anger that may be unrelated to any specific influence or interference. This anger can be continuous even when there is nothing apparent to incite it. This general feeling of anger keeps you under stress, which can be released explosively. It may be slow, building to the point of overt expression, but the release can be spontaneous and intense.

While the elimination of the temper tic through the trait of directness applies only in certain structures, you can benefit from the direct approach, which does not allow for psychological involvement that can hamper intelligent functioning.

ARGUMENTATIVENESS:

Indicated when the stem of the letter p rises above the circular part of the letter. The higher the stem extends, the stronger the trait. If the stem is also looped, your imagination will play a part in your arguing. You will call upon every source imaginable to make your point.

Note: The lower loop does not apply. It may be either looped or retraced. Let it remain as it wishes.

Argumentativeness is another resistance. It comes from a fear of not being able to defend yourself if you are challenged, if your ideas meet with rejection, when you find yourself in controversy. You are always on alert to the possibility, real or unreal, of being questioned. You resist before a challenge has been presented, and it may never be presented; you expect others to oppose you. You anticipate confrontation and are always prepared psychologically, but your resistance can outrun your logic.

Argumentativeness is opposed to reasonable debate. Although it is not essential to do so, if you start the first stroke of the letter at the top of the circle part of the letter, or the middle zone, and not above it, and move directly down through the baseline and on below to form the lower zone of the letter, you omit the approach stroke often associated with this tension-provoking and energy-wasting trait.

The trait of directness does not, per se, eliminate argumentativeness, but it tends to discourage it. With all of the assets already instilled, you do not need to resist psychologically. Your mind is clear to function well when challenged.

This trait can be evidenced within a word as well as at the beginning of a word. As mentioned in Chapter Six, directness can free the mind to accept the spontaneous spark of intuition that is eager to come to the aid of your thinking.

p p p

pet pat

apt pure

prepare

pie pick

keep

apple

Practice Assignment:

Practice structures separately that indicate directness. Incorporate them into words, phrases and sentences, always using the traits assimilated since the beginning of this study. This stroke can also appear within words.

Many words, phrases and sentences may be used to practice our trait we call directness

Practice Page

Please change only the structures you have already studied.
Do not attempt or force any other alterations.

h
g
k
y
b
f
m
n
n
a
d
o
g
s
i
t

a
b
c
d
e
f
g
h
i
k
m
n
o
r
s
t
y
g
s

Jane, an attractive mother, came with her 11 year old daughter, Judy. After her analysis, Jane exclaimed enthusiastically, "You know everything about me! Are you sure you don't live in my house?" As I was analyzing Judy's writing, Jane glanced skeptically, several times between Judy and me, then interrupted, "You're all wrong about Judy. You were absolutely right about me. . . , but you're way off with Judy." Even when Judy shyly nodded her head to let her mother know that it was true, Jane continued to deny it. As they left, the mother still didn't believe her daughter. Judy knew the truth, but had hidden her psychological fears so well that she appeared poised, mature and well adjusted, even to her mother.

"Too swift arrives as tardy as too slow."
William Shakespeare

"Wise to resolve, and patient to perform."
Alexander Pope

"Every man's memory is his private literature."
Aldous Huxley

CHAPTER TWELVE
Your I-Dots

The manner in which you execute your *i*-dots reveals these characteristics: sense of timing, your ability to schedule activities and to function in accord with the schedule; observation of details, your capacity to notice minute details; the manner in which you handle details; patience, your capacity to maintain a sense of calm despite outside influences; mental memory, the capacity to remember factual information. (Emotional, sensuous memory was discussed in Chapter 2.)

- Are you usually on time?

- Are you often late?

- Do you act impulsively?

- Do you procrastinate?

- Are you observant?

- Do you remember facts and dates?

- Are you comfortable delegating details?

- Do you trust only yourself with details?

- Do you feel patient?

My Personal Handwriting

Write down the things in your life that are most irritating to you.

- Do you feel irritable?

- Do you have minor, or major, accidents?

- Do you want to improve your game?

SENSE OF TIMING:

Indicated by placement of *i*-dots in a direct line with the stem of the letter. This gives you the capacity to schedule details and activities and to handle them in accord with your scheduling. You have your individual speed of functioning. If your inner rate of speed is slow, you need to allot extra time for unexpected interruptions, because you cannot hurry to compensate for the time lost in handling them. If your inner speed is fast, you often feel tempted to act impulsively and reduce your efficiency. When your i-dots are precisely in line with the stem, you are moving in coordination with your inner speed and your scheduling. You are not acting impulsively nor are you irrationally procrastinating. Also, you have good physical coordination. You don't swing your racquet or club too fast or too slowly. You don't bump into corners or stumble up curbs.

Your speed of functioning may have changed constructively since you began your study.

PROCRASTINATION:

Indicated by the placement of i-dots to the left of the stem. This is procrastination in handling details. You are putting off what you think you should be doing or what you have scheduled for yourself. This affects you psychologically. You haven't given yourself permission to delay a matter. This type of procrastination will cause your body to move too slowly. Your psychological lag induces physical lag. Your awareness of what you believe to be your dilatory behavior can then promote impulsiveness, so that you move too fast, ahead of schedule. Impulsiveness can also promote procrastination.

IMPULSIVE BEHAVIOR:

in Time

Timing

in Time

Timing

Timing

in Time

Timing

in Time

Timing

in Time

Indicated by the placement of i-dots to the right of the stem. The farther to the right, the stronger the trait.

You are moving too fast, being impulsive, acting before you think. This can happen regardless of your inner speed, which may be fast, slow or varied. You feel an impulse to act immediately, not giving full heed to all the consequences. You can also feel pressure from people and circumstances to hurry to suit their plans and desires. With correctly placed *i*-dots you can hurry more efficiently, and lessen the risk of accidents.

When you move too fast inwardly, your body will move too fast. You can also plan impulsively. You may want to do ten things, but you don't consider, logically, that it might not be possible. If you plan rationally, knowing you may not be able to accomplish everything, your handwriting will not be affected.

Impulsiveness and procrastination can appear in the same handwriting. For instance, if you don't realize you have planned impulsively, when all is not done, you can believe you have procrastinated. This shows in the handwriting, and the procrastination will cause your body to move too slowly.

While impulsiveness and procrastination can be mutual inducements, this is not necessarily so. Some of you may never procrastinate, but behave impulsively. Some never behave impulsively, but procrastinate. It is interesting to note that intentional "procrastination" may never show in the handwriting. When you decide, logically, to put off doing something, for any reason whatsoever, when you are not affected emotionally or psychologically by what you or others may judge as your indolence, the trait of procrastination does not appear in your writing.

Accurate timing is a safety device. In precise manual work, in any activity in which body movement is important, in driving, sports, dancing, in working with machinery, you are not likely to have accidents that are due to your own irregular timing.

Note: You can move rapidly and not be impulsive.
You can move slowly without procrastinating.

OBSERVATION OF DETAILS: (Affects mental memory)

Indicated by the distance of the *i*-dot from the stem of the *i*. This reveals how closely you observe and attend to details.

When your *i*-dots are very close, you see everything, the most minute detail doesn't escape your eye. You usually prefer handling details yourself because you feel others may not take care of them properly. You can be called a "nit-picker." The farther from the stem, the more likely you are to delegate details, or handle them with less compunction.

If your work requires you to do fine, detailed work, close *i*-dots can be an asset. If you need to assign details, or if you are involved simultaneously in a variety of activities, your *i*-dots may be well-placed higher above the stem. They must always be in line with the stem.

I-dots near the stem also indicate that you are more likely to remember what you have learned or observed. You have put your attention on it closely enough to fasten it in your mind. You can have a good mental memory and a poor sensuous memory, and vice versa.

When, however, you feel impatient or irritable, even with your *i*-dots placed very close to the stem, you may forget what you have seen because your attention has been shaken away by your feeling of impatience or irritability. These traits can also cause you to dismiss, neglect, or attend to details with less than your best efforts.

than your best efforts.

patience

quiet

simple

impatient is

irritable is

impatience

this is it

PATIENCE AND IRRITABILITY:

Patience is indicated by quiet, unmoving, simple *i*-dots, regardless of the distance from the stem.

The more jagged and/or slashed the dots, the more impatient and irritable you feel. (This does not mean that you are angry with a specific person or situation. The irritability is within you.) As you jab at the paper with your pencil, you become more irritated; you are fighting the fire with the fuel that sparked it. Your impatience automatically puts pressure on your mind, causing it to be jarred away from the thought at hand, distracting your mind from the purpose of your thinking.

Some can behave patiently even when feeling impatient and irritable. You may act with outer calm while inwardly you are champing at the bit. Impatience and irritability waste and misuse your energy and can further aggravate the mental and emotional discomfort that has promoted it. It can also affect you physically. The quiet, precisely placed *i*-dot is an indication of your inner attitude of patience. I-dots directly in line with the stem indicate the ability to schedule accurately and function in sync with your inner rate of speed, and your intended schedule.

Since all traits must be evaluated with all others, a patient person can have traits that can cause a blowup. With all your previous study, however, this is not likely to happen.

NOTE: *I-dots executed in the shape of circles, hearts, X's or other idiosyncratic formations may indicate patience but are not to your benefit. They indicate your need to receive special attention for your own special work performed by your own special self. This requirement for "special-ness" comes from fear of not being recognized as a special individual. Now that you have achieved your integrated self, you do not need to be singled out as unique.*

Practice Assignment:

Practice *i*'s, *j*'s and periods with well-placed and well-formed dots, separately and in words, phrases and sentences using the expertise you have heretofore achieved.

Practice Page

Please change only the structures you have already studied.
Do not attempt or force any other alterations.

h
g
k
y
b
f
m
n
n
a
d
o
g
s
i
t

a
b
c
d
e
f
g
h
i
k
m
n
o
r
s
t
y
g
s

"The measure of man is what he does with his power."
        Pittacus (650?-560? B.C.)

"Greatness lies not in being strong, but in the right use of strength."
        Henry Ward Beecher

"I have never been able to conceive how any rational being could propose happiness to himself from the exercise of power over others."
        Thomas Jefferson

"Power dements even more than it corrupts, lowering the guard of foresight and raising the haste of action."
        Will and Ariel Durant

"As for men in power, they are so anxious to establish the myth of infallibility that they do their utmost to ignore truth."
        Boris Pasternak

"All cruelty springs from weakness".
        Seneca

CHAPTER THIRTEEN
Energy Toward Goals— Will-Force

With all of your previous study and practice, you are now prepared to consider your will-force, its consistency and durability necessary to keep you on the path toward your major goal. Will-force has to do with the magnetism between you and your goal. In the next chapter we will discuss the kinds of goals that are important to you. In this chapter we are discussing how you extend your energy toward your goals.

Are you planning and carrying through with your plan, or are you distracted by immediate demands? Does your temper, your blaming others, drag you into unnecessary, irrelevant pursuits? Do you assume responsibility for your own success, or do you resort to dominating and domineering others, trying to force them to use their energies for you? Does frustration drain your energy? Are you sarcastic in your criticism?

We will deal here with both constructive and wasteful uses of energy. On one hand you have your will-force, enthusiasm, planning and scheduling ability. On the other, there is procrastination, temper, dominating and domineering attitudes and behavior.

My Personal Handwriting
Write about what makes you angry.

WILL FORCE/POWER:

Indicated by t-bars, or t-crossings, that are as heavy as the stem of the letter *t*.

By far the most constructive use of will force occurs when the pressure of the *t*-bar, i.e. the weight, the heaviness, of the stroke, is consistent from the beginning of the stroke to the end and is equal to that of the stem of the letter. This shows that the energy and the follow-through of energy are directed consistently and appropriately toward your goal.

SARCASM:

Indicated in t-bars that feather or fade away.

When your *t*-bars feather out, fade away, your energy and will-force also fade. You feel frustrated. You can be annoyed with immediate problems and lose sight of your major goal. Your frustration drains your energy and drive to succeed. If you express your discontent it will be with a sharp, sarcastic bite. With *t*-bars of consistent pressure, or energy, you are maintaining your drive and interest in your goal, and are automatically eliminating the trait of sarcasm.

Since you have followed the chapter on generosity, none of your strokes will be fading. They will be continuing with the same strength from beginning to end.

With this constant energy, you have also increased your capacity to plan and carry through.

PLANNING ABILITY:

t̶ time at̶

⟷ ⟷

This quality is seen in *t*-bars of consistent pressure, continuing with the same strength from beginning to end, and are the same length on either side of the stem. It is the capacity to plan and keep your will-force directed consistently and on schedule toward your goals.

SENSE OF TIMING REGARDING GOALS:

This is indicated by the *t*-bars balancing on the stem, being of equal length on either side, as above.

It is the ability to carry through with your overall plan according to your prescribed schedule. When you have this sense of timing, it automatically eliminates procrastination about your goals. Immediate circumstances may require your immediate attention, but your major goal maintains its long-range magnetism.

PROCRASTINATION IN MAJOR GOALS:

Time

to

start

time

Indicated by t-bars that are longer to the left of the stem or that are placed to the left. The farther to the left, the stronger the degree of procrastination.

This is procrastination about major activities having to do with your own most important personal goals and, in some cases, the goals of others to whom you have made a commitment.

You can become involved in your present activity instead of moving ahead with your planned agenda. You can forsake your personal, long-range goals and concede to the pressure of someone else's goal, or to a common goal, or to one that is merely whimsical fancy, as opposed to your major one.

Procrastination in *t*-bars can also be due to boredom with unchallenging activity, it can be laziness, it can be that you have allowed an immediate impulse or desire to distract you from a commitment to a task, or it can be a worthy demand-of the-moment, an unexpected responsibility.

TEMPER/ANGER:

Indicated by t-bars that are longer, or are placed completely, to the right of the stem.

With this trait you are angry with an environment you feel is obstructing your progress. If your t-bars are consistently to the right, you are feeling consistently upset with people and situations and are always prepared to fight back at the slightest, even imagined or preconceived provocation. You may possibly not expose this anger, or you can feel it when there is no obvious reason to be upset. Your temper causes you to be impulsive, to jump irrationally ahead of, or away from, your schedule, from what you are doing. In your haste you waste time and energy. When your temper blasts off, your intelligence also takes leave. You cannot be under the influence of your temper and simultaneously think rationally. Temper is anticipating that the world is attacking you, acting as your enemy, and you are prepared to open fire.

The farther to the right, and the longer and heavier the stroke, the stronger and longer-lasting the fit of temper. The intensity of this mindless experience can result in tremendous inner pressure and outward release; your energy is directed, focused, toward a threat that can be nonexistent--and if it does exist, you have lost your capacity to deal with it realistically, rationally or philosophically.

When the bar slants downward, your temper is intended to strike out against and hurt anyone you feel is intruding upon you and your efforts. It is "their fault that I'm angry, they made me mad, they deserve my wrath."

It is possible to have t-bars that are the same length on either side and experience a buildup of pressures that can result in blowing up--the lid flying off. This is not temper as described here, though it may seem so. You are not angry with anyone. There can be a slight and perhaps unrelated "straw" that releases the pressure. It can, in some cases, be a violent release, a loss of control. This happens more often with a perpendicular slant and low philosophical stroke.

With the other traits you have developed, the pressures are much less likely to build and need release, inasmuch as they are vanquished before they occur. And other qualities, as mentioned in Chapter 2, have automatically been beneficially altered, as needed.

When you are angry, your body as well as your emotions can move too fast. An overall sense of timing, in regard to both details, and goals, is of great benefit in preventing accidents.

Temper is a waste of energy and can cause emotional and physical discomfort as well as harm to a relationship, to others, to projects, and to yourself. It is an enemy to joyful and intelligent living.

EXCESSIVE BLUNT WILL:

When a *t*-bar grows stronger, and ends bluntly instead of remaining the same, the will grows in intensity as difficulties are encountered or desires thwarted.

When this happens your driving force clogs. This, also, is misused energy; it is not needed when you are functioning constructively as you are training yourself to do. You are working toward consistent energy, rather than energy that accelerates, slows or stops because of psychological fears, resistances or escapes.

DOMINEERING:

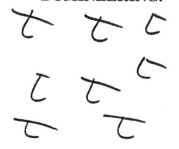

Indicated if your t-bar moves downward and also fades. This is a domineering attitude that requires others to accomplish your goals for you and that blames them if you fail. You look upon failure as "theirs," and success as "yours." At the same time you are domineering them into making you successful. You can abuse others in an attempt to credit yourself.

You are not using your own intelligence to achieve your own goals. This results from fear of not succeeding on your own ability; you credit others with failure and yourself with success. You feel you deserve to have power over others.

There is also a kind of laziness, and an attitude of pessimism, involved; you are afraid you can't achieve your goal and want to force others to do it for you. There is a sudden loss of energy that demands that it be replaced by someone else's. This makes a difficult situation for others, both personally and professionally.

When you have this trait, you are not taking your share of responsibility for achieving personal and professional goals--nor for failure in reaching them--and when you punish, with words, silence or some kind of deprivation, it is with whip and rapier. You feel you are in command and fearless because you are playing the role of dictator.

The manner in which you accomplish your end depends upon other traits. And, as you are now in command of your strengths, this trait, if it had been a part of your handwriting, may have disappeared. It is to your advantage to recognize it and understand it.

DOMINATING:

Indicated by t-bars that slant down and do not fade out but maintain consistent pressure to the end.

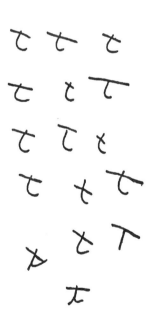

This trait means that you are trying to control your environment so that it will follow the prescribed plan. You are in control, the puppeteer. You do not ask others to do your job, as in domineering, nor do you blame them necessarily. But you demand that they do the tasks that you have assigned to them.

If the bar grows heavier at the end, you are excessively demanding. When you strike out, it is with a club.

The need to dominate comes from a fear that your plan will not be fulfilled. You are feeling depressed and pessimistic about your progress. This is a waste of energy that could be used more appropriately in leading than in overpowering. It can cause those working under you, or with you, to feel over-supervised, and possibly resent or resist in some way.

SHALLOW PURPOSE:

this that

the truth

trait tan

ta to

take twee

Indicated by concave *t*-bars; they dish in, scoop downward.

If you have *t*-bars that qualify, you are directing energies toward insignificant goals. These *t*-bars reveal a shallowness of purpose that can involve fear of failure, boredom, ignorance of, or lack of interest in, valuable goals. Also, you may be substituting an expedient, or irrelevant, immediate goal for your long-range one, and thus reduce the possibility of achieving what you want most. Your minor, and often misconceived, goals become major ones.

Shallow goals can also be destructive ones, such as certain manners of over-indulging sensuous, or psychological needs.

When you place your *t*-bars evenly on the stem, with consistent, even weight or pressure throughout, and do not dish in or slant downward, you use your energy consistently and well, and you have the ability to move steadily forward, carrying out plans according to schedule, towards your goal.

ENTHUSIASM:

enthusiastic

Time it

enthusiasm

toward

this time

Indicated by long *t*-bars. The longer the t-bar, the longer lasting the will-force, drive, and enthusiasm toward your goal. There is, however, a point beyond which more enthusiasm is expended than is needed or healthful. When your *t*-bars extend longer than the space required by five of your letters, your enthusiasm may exceed your need; you can feel enervated as you put out more mental, emotional and physical energy toward your goals than is efficient.

OPTIMISM:

Indicated by *t*-bars that rise, or slant upward.

This shows an optimistic attitude toward your goals; obstacles do not long depress you, drag you down.

When you own these constructive traits as revealed in your *t*-bars, you find that everything works more effectively. You apply these characteristics to all goals, both short and long-range, either material or philosophical ones.

Practice Assignment:

Form *t*-bars consistent with the foregoing description and add them to the practice of other strokes in words, phrases and sentences.

As you progress through your study and practice, you will find it easier to acquire constructive characteristics. Some of them may have come of their own accord, without conscious effort on your part.

Practice Page

**Please change only the structures you have already studied.
Do not attempt or force any other alterations.**

h
g
k
y
b
f
m
n
n
a
d
o
g
s
i
t

a
b
c
d
e
f
g
h
i
k
m
n
o
r
s
t
y
z

An eighty-one year old woman was helped with the practice of grapho-therapy. She had suffered from migraine headaches all of her adult life, and found that they disappeared after eliminating the stress of irrational worry and repression by changing her handwriting.

"One is left with remorse that his life could not be concentrated on its proper goal."
                    Dadu

"We must ask where we are and whither we are tending."
                    Abraham Lincoln

"We...repeatedly enlarge our instrumentalities without improving our purpose."
                    Will Durant

"If one advances confidently in the direction of his dreams, and endeavors to live the life which he has imagined, he will meet with a success unexpected in common hours."
                    Henry David Thoreau

"Why not spend some time in determining what is worthwhile for us, and then go after that?"
                    William Ross

CHAPTER FOURTEEN
Setting Goals— Self-Confidence

N
ow, with your new awareness and understanding, when you look at your handwriting, you can see for yourself the concrete evidence indicating that, among other achievements, you:

- are an integrated person, a well balanced individual with a sense of equanimity.

- have recovered full use of your inner consciousness, your abstract capacity.

- can deal with people and situations realistically.

- have a consistent flow of energy.

- own that precious commodity, generosity.

- can communicate fearlessly, accurately, sincerely, kindly, with both yourself and others.

- can organize, using both your conceptual and material imagination.

- can think logically, creatively, intuitively.

- are patient.

- know the value of assistance, but do not expect others to submit to your demands.

- can appropriately lead, follow, or share the path toward goals.

- can discover the scope of life's opportunities.

- can direct your energy toward ultimate goals.

- are prepared to secure a valid self-confidence that has no fear of failure, with the confidence to strive toward your utmost desire.

What is "utmost" to you may not be utmost, or even understandable, to the less integrated. You now know that the most practical way and the ideal way are one and the same. You take a practical view toward any goal, even visionary ones. Why waste time and energy struggling through the silt and muck of the river bed when you can swim in the clear water at the top of the river? You tackle both present and distant goals with the same ease.

SELF-CONFIDENCE:

Indicated by *t*-bars that are placed high on the stem, from three-quarters the height of the stem to the top.

This is self-confidence, fearlessness in setting your goals in accord with your highest aspirations and good judgment. Fear of failure is not an issue.

T-bars placed mid-way or lower on the stem show fear of failure, self-underestimation, refusal to put faith in your ability. You accept others' evaluation of you and your capacity to succeed in achieving your favorite goals.

Please remember that these high *t*-bars must be accompanied with balance and your previous study or they can work to your disadvantage. You can feel dissatisfied, even discouraged and without direction.

True self-confidence is not arrogant, does not boast, "I can do anything I want." It is the essence of bold humility.

Your individual integrity tells you to devote your efforts and energy toward that which you now realize is valuable to you. You will not be mired down by any stultifying fears, and the goals the world sets for you.

You can choose your goals and work toward them with renewed intelligence. You understand that high self-confidence and strong will-force can be misused, can do more harm than good, if other characteristics are not available to support and assist them in selecting and traveling toward well-set goals.

With your philosophic outlook you know that you can lay bricks or design skyscrapers, be artist or woodsman, homemaker, teacher or physician; you know that no occupation can, of itself, bring either joy or sorrow, success or failure.

You know that true pleasure in life, a sense of personal security, serenity, and vigor, is internal and can be experienced fully only by an integrated human being.

Along with establishing major goals, you give yourself the capacity to recognize and handle everyday goals and responsibilities within a total perspective. You are not obsessed or distracted by mundane activities. They do not chain your spirit. You can deal with them practically, with a good, whole, and lightened heart.

Practice Assignment:

Practice many *t*-bars. Use them in words, phrases and sentences. If some ending *t*'s are formed as shown in fig. A, you may continue to use the structure, and use the usual *t* formation elsewhere.

title This

to that

it

Fig. A

Employing all the characteristics learned previously, incorporate the self-confidence *t*-bars, in paragraphs of writing. Practice all structures until they come easily. Enjoy all you have developed.

Practice Page

Please change only the structures you have already studied.
Do not attempt or force any other alterations.

h
g
k
y
b
f
m
n
n
a
d
o
g
s
i
t

a
b
c
d
e
f
g
h
i
k
m
n
o
r
s
t
y
g
s

DEMANDING SENSUOUS DESIRES

A man in his mid-thirties had been in group therapy for three years. His writing showed that he was yielding to every persuading force around him, and was giving in to his own powerful sensuous desires. His philosophical capacity was limited; his need to be loved, respected and appreciated was excessive. (He had been buffeted about among orphanages and foster homes). He felt wrenched apart. The outcome was his irresponsible and harmful behavior toward others and himself. He now says he feels he knows where he is going and is developing the capacity to get there. He understands the motivations behind his unacceptable behavior and is directing himself toward the higher goals that he has chosen intelligently, as opposed to the former ones determined by his compulsion to fight back, to satisfy demands of the senses, and to be recognized as someone to whom attention must be paid.

CHAPTER FIFTEEN
Saying "Yes" and "No"

Do you say "Yes" and then wish you'd said "No?"

Do you give in for no good reason?

You are equipped with all the qualities necessary for using good judgment.

This is a final touch. It protects you from yielding your judgment illogically to others. With this stroke you give yourself full permission to say "yes" or "no" with due consideration to the consequences, instead of submitting to the path of least resistance.

You guard yourself against the temptation to give in to your emotional impulse to yield, submit, give in to irrational influences, in order to avoid disharmony.

Actually the yielding can create as much disharmony as it avoids.

With this trait you can still choose to adjust to accommodate a person or situation in an appropriate way, but when you "yield," you will do so from choice rather than compulsion.

If, however, you do not own your own integrity, this trait can augment selfishness, domineering, or any other undesirable trait.

You are adding this capacity to enhance the natural resources you have nurtured.

YIELDING IRRATIONALLY;

this is

sample

this is

sample

sample

This trait is indicated by a soft, rolling s. Giving in, saying "yes," unreasonably.

In a sudden thrust of emotion, you tumble head over heels to please, to accede to another's wishes, or to indulge your own self in some way that is out of accord with what you really want, and that could be detrimental to you. It can also make an unpleasant combination with other traits.

NON-YIELDING;

sample

is this

is this

sample is

sons so

says as

Is indicated when your *s* is sharp, pointed at the top. With this stroke, you are choosing to say "yes" or "no" based on your best judgment. The mind is working crisply in making the choice. You are not giving in compulsively.

The direct, printed-type *s* is also unyielding. It must, however, be the same height as surrounding, middle-zone structures, and the final stroke must move forward to the right. As was mentioned earlier, all final strokes must move forward.

Practice Assignment:

Add this structure to the limitless number of combinations of structures in words, phrases, sentences, paragraphs. Give free rein to creativity and inventiveness.

Enjoy the process of being yourself. Enjoy yourself.

Practice Page

Please change only the structures you have already studied.
Do not attempt or force any other alterations.

h
g
k
y
b
f
m
n
n
a
d
o
g
s
i
t

a
b
c
d
e
f
g
h
i
k
m
n
o
r
s
t
y
z

CHAPTER SIXTEEN
Signatures

Incorporate all of the characteristics you have developed into your signature.

Occasionally signatures are written differently from the body of the writing. Whatever the individual reasons are for doing this, the differences represent inner conflict. By the time you have arrived at this point in your study, your signatures and the rest of your writing may be similar. If they are not, you can make the proper adjustments.

The height of the initial letters of your names should not be taller than your abstract loops in the body of your writing.

Initials that exceed the height of your philosophical loops are indicative of an exaggerated need for ego recognition. This is, of course, a fear of not being recognized as an admirable, worthwhile individual. It is a vain effort to adorn yourself in a coat of splendor, to be better received by others, and yourself. This, as with the tall *d*'s and *t*'s, can come across to others as braggadocio. Now, with your accomplishments in self-graphotherapy, you have become yourself and have no need for such aggrandizement.

SIGNATURES OF
WELL-KNOWN PEOPLE

Walt Disney

Paul Revere

Gerald R. Ford

Jacqueline Kennedy

A Lincoln

Henry Ford

Henry Miller

Jack London

Richard Nixon

CHAPTER SEVENTEEN

YOUR

and

MANUAL DEXTERITY AND ARTISTIC APTITUDE
as seen in the way you form your letter r

Those individuals who have elected to develop the traits of manual dexterity and artistic aptitude, as indicated in the letter *r,* have found that their thought processes have improved in structure and that their personal pleasure in beauty has increased. Both of these aptitudes may be found in the same handwriting. (These traits may be indicated elsewhere in the handwriting but the letter *r* serves this purpose.)

Manual dexterity, per se, as seen in the letter *r*, is often present in the handwriting of engineers, drummers, (nearly always in rock and roll drummers), potters, sculptures, commercial artists, in mechanics, contractors, builders, farmers, plumbers, truck drivers, etc.

MANUAL DEXTERITY:
The ability to use one's hands capably and surely, is indicated in the letter *r* that is flat, square, on top.

The handwriting of those whose occupations are mentioned above may also reveal the extended trait of artistic aptitude.

Artistic or cultural aptitude, can also include manual dexterity, the flat area in the letter *r*. It is an inclination toward the arts in their highest form, and is often found in the handwriting of classical musicians, and in jazz scholars, in fine artists, poets, the finest designers, decorators, floral arrangers, etc., or in one who simply appreciates beauty beyond its purely sensuous value, who will make something beautiful out of un-beautiful surroundings. With this trait you are more likely to be able to discern quality. Such beauty, recognized, has been known to have a healing effect.

ARTISTIC APTITUDE,

as seen in the letter *r*, gives somewhat the impression of a Greek *e*. The formation may contain two curves, and may include the flat area of manual dexterity.

The first stroke, rising higher, shows the mind's inclination to reach above the mundane, its interest being directed not only toward the product created, but toward its less tangible values.

A lack of evidence of these traits in your handwriting does not mean that you are not learned or skilled in a particular area. It usually means that if you have them you are not using these aptitudes to your own personal satisfaction.

If you are knowledgeable, or have performed in activities requiring these aptitudes, and they are not present in your handwriting, you could easily have developed a resistance to an environment that seems to be restricting your appreciation of, and/or engagement in such endeavors. (This resistance is indicated when your *r* is printed or larger than other middle zone letters.) A longing to use your latent talents can arise, and you may feel like bursting the bonds that tie you down. As you know, any resistance is a hindrance to your intelligent functioning.

When you build, or rebuild, these aptitudes into your handwriting you can be spared the frustration of circumstances that limit your talents or skills.

Whether or not these traits are necessary to psychological health, whether or not you choose to use them, they can contribute to your thought patterns, and enhance your day-to-day enjoyment.

Practice Assignment:

You may practice these strokes as you have previous ones, until they are a part of you.

A fifty year old man, recovering from a severe heart condition credited his two graphotherapy sessions with saving his life. He worked professionally in health services.

EXPERIENCES OF SOME WHO HAVE
USED THIS PROCESS

Donald was wondering what directions he wanted to take, in both his personal and professional life. He was being hurt by the criticism from his family and friends, all of whom he felt he needed to please. Their respect was vital to him.

(Sample of writing on his first visit)

I acknowledge that this is a sample of my handwriting.

Within a few weeks he had made those decisions, and his family and friends were treating him with respect. They were approving of him, of his abilities and his decisions.

(Sample of writing on his last visit)

is a sample of my handwriting.

Kathy felt at a loss about many things, including herself, her family and her creative endeavors.

(Sample of her writing on her first visit)

I know this is a sample of my handwriting

After two weeks she said, "I feel wonderful, but I don't understand; it seems like magic".

(Sample of her writing after two weeks)

I know that this is a sample of my handwriting
I know that this is a sample of my handwriting

Tom wanted to make a decision about going into business for himself. The members of his family had their own differing ideas.

(Sample of his writing on his first visit)

I acknowledge this to be a sample of my handwriting
Signed

After a few weeks he said, "I can see the light at the end of the tunnel and hope to get life running smoothly again within a very short time", which he did.

(Sample of his writing on his last visit)

I acknowledge this to be a sample of my handwriting

Signed

Margot's life was fraught with enormous and varied problems. She came for graphotherapy, "confused, tired...I felt like a wisp. I wasn't sleeping and hadn't the faintest idea what to do." Her pressure was almost too light to be seen and nearly impossible to copy. (Due to printing limitations this writing printed heavier than the original).

(Sample of her writing on her first visit)

I might be able to use in a future job so that I feel more independant.

After one week she said that her husband remarked about how well organized she was, and that she had finally enjoyed a night's sleep. Now she says, "I have been able to handle all of my family's problems, cheerfully! My own health has as improved, and with everything that's going on I've developed a business of my own at home".

(Sample of her writing after a few weeks)

I acknowledge that this is a sample of my handwriting

Elizabeth, on her first visit wrote, "I want my life to slow down. I want to grow - I want to give - I want to become. I want to be free, to be who I was meant to be. I don't want anything or anybody to stop me from that which wants to come out of me. I want to be allowing my creativeness to emerge. I want my love to flow unhindered.

I love my family - my two daughters, but I've found only pain and struggles in my home.

I can best describe my home a stagnant place - a crowded place - no chance to grow to develop.

My bedroom is a room of tears. My children's room is so cramped - they fight all the time and I feel so very helpless. My strength is always depleted by the time I get home from giving all day at school. What's left of me is usually irritable, cross and hysterical.

I want to laugh, have fun, feel silly and free, but life for me is too serious, so full of fears that I feel paralyzed.

We never have people over. My husband has never once brought home a friend. All our friends are my contacts. I usually socialize with them outside our home."

(This is a sample of her first writing)

I acknowledge this is a sample of my handwriting.
Kathy
I acknowledge this is a sample of my handwriting.
Kathy

(A later sample of her writing)

I acknowledge this is a sample of my handwriting.

During a later visit Elizabeth wrote, "I have been enjoying my daily writing practice. It makes me feel real good inside. Somehow that good feeling stayed with me throughout the day.

I waited to see if this would last or go away. The pressure began to mount, but I still felt amazingly balanced within myself.

My family noticed this too. They are watching to see when mother will loose her cool. They have responded positively to my relaxed attitude.

My daughter and I had some delightful days together while my other daughter was away on her trip. I was so glad to spend some quality time with her, who sometimes feels neglected.

My husband feels more relaxed around me. He hopes this will last."

continued

RESPONSES FROM SOME WHO HAVE
EXPERIENCED SELF-GRAPHO THERAPY

Ms. Mary Dawn Gladson,

Just a note to tell you how much I appreciate the grapho-therapy that I received from you. Since practicing the various strokes you gave me, my timing has been better; communications with others have improved; concentration and memory are significantly enhanced; and I'm able to take criticism without having my feelings hurt, just to mention some obvious changes.

I know that this is all the result of the analysis you made of my handwriting and then correcting my different strokes to benefit all the above. It has certainly made a difference in my life and you can be assured that I'm sharing this with all my friends, who have commented on my improved behavior. I wish there were a book that I could refer to, though, instead of calling you, when I seem to need some additional assistance.

Thank you, Mary Dawn, for all that you have done for me; it is greatly appreciated.

Best personal regards,
/s/ Rosemary Montana-Penland

GRAPHOTHERAPY WORKS!

May I introduce you to Anicia Caulfield of November 1978. She was a graduate student in music with a full-time unit load. She also worked 25-30 hours per week as an office manager and systems analyst for a small mini-computer company. But most importantly, Anicia's handwriting at this time was showing signs of inner frustration, repression, lots of fear and worry, and physical weakness.

The point of collapse had just happened several weeks earlier. The diagnosis, after many hours of lab tests, was severe hypoglycemia, related stomach disorders, chronic anemia and sinusitis. As an overachiever, Anicia had finally blown a fuse and lost her most important asset, her health. Her handwriting showed many positive traits, but the under estimation of self and constant barrage of negative feelings about herself that Anicia had been actively promoting were the main reasons for the final collapse physically, thus allowing all the above illnesses freedom to appear and play havoc on Anicia's system.

Then Anicia was introduced to a grapho-analyst for one hour. Immediate exercises were assigned that almost instantly improved

Anicia's energy levels. Exercises for redoing some bad writing habits helped to eliminate inner feelings of resentment, sarcasm, fear and worry. Emphasis was placed on strengthening the many positive traits already present in Anicia's handwriting. And surprisingly, with a little bit of daily effort, progress was being noted.

Communication with peers, faculty, parents and others came much easier. Self confidence and respect become evident with more attention being shown to personal appearance, proper rest and diet and healthy thinking habits. Being a generous person, Anicia was finally learning her limits, physically and mentally. She could now say "No" without the heavy burden of self guilt and deprivation. She also had the strength physically to finish her semester at school maintaining high grades and doing well at her job. Most importantly, Anicia was over-coming the long list of physical ailments she had in November.

The new year saw Anicia heading for a new job, a college grant and whole new outlook on life. Her handwriting had improved to the point where only small signs of worry, repression and physical weakness were present. These had mainly been replaced with a willingness to communicate, a balance of logic and emotions, a strengthening of self confidence and lots of humor and enthusiasm. Physically, Anicia had been making great strides, only having the problem of hypoglycemia left on her list.

Exercises were now assigned to strengthen the prevalent positive traits, to even out the fluctuation of energy and emotions and to eliminate the last traces of repression and worry. With only 20-30 minutes of daily writing, very little expense, and lots of encouragement, Anicia again made progress.

Yes, graphotherapy works! The Anicia of today is strong, happy, and very healthy. She has practiced her writing without tremendous amounts of conscious effort, counseling or expense. In the last six months the time investment has been minimal compared to what it could have been driving to doctors, waiting for their advice, and shopping for their prescriptions. Twenty to thirty minutes a day devoted to a very simple and even enjoyable therapy has been the major contributing factor to Anicia's current health and improved outlook on life. Last week the diagnosis was that of being 90% cured.

Self-Graphotherapy works! -- just ask anyone who knew the Anicia of 1978!!

Happily and with health restored,

/s/ Anicia Caulfield
(Written in 1979)

ABOUT FREEDOM

We have used the words, <u>freedom</u> and <u>free</u>, repeatedly throughout the pages of this book and were delighted to find a scholarly reference to the effect that, historically, their meaning has been less bound up with the sometimes sterile connotation of "going it alone" -- an emphasis acquired in recent centuries -- than with the idea of living productively with one's neighbors. During the greater part of history in the Indo-European world, the word <u>freedom</u> applied to men and women who lived in peace and love with one another.

"Free: . . . cf. (Old Norse) <u>frithr</u>, love, peace; (old English) <u>frithu</u>; (Old High German) <u>fridu</u>, peace; (Gothic) <u>frijon</u>, to love: or remotely yet significantly (Sanskrit) <u>priyas</u>, beloved, and <u>private</u>, he loves."*

You have established an integrity that frees you to face with equanimity anything and everything that life has to offer. You will easily recognize any disturbing reactions you may experience and dispense with them through the use of the principles you know how to apply. Your extension of your higher freedom is limitless.

---

* Eric Partridge, <u>Origins: A Short Etymological Dictionary of Modern English</u>. New York: Greenwich House, 1983.

VARIED SAMPLES OF HANDWITING

This is a sample of
my handwriting

This is
a sample of
my handwriting

This is a sample of
my handwriting

Jay

This is a sample of my handwriting.

this is a sample of
my handwriting

This is a sample of
my handwriting.

This is a sample of
my handwriting!

handwriting like

This is a sample of of my

my handwriting. This is a sample
my handwriting

This is a sample of
my handwriting. This is a sample
of my handwriting,

This is a sample of of my
my handwriting.

This is a sample
of my handwriting

this is a sample of my handwriting

this is a sample Know this is
of my handwriting handwri

This is a sample
of my handwriting

This is a sample of my handwriting.

This is a sample of my handwriting

This is a sample of my handwriting

Know this is a sample my handwriting.

Know this is

this is a sample My handwritin

This is a Sample of my Handwriting

This is a sample of my handwriting

This is a sample of My Handwriting

my Handwriting

my handwriting

This is a sample of my handwriting

This is a sample of my
handwriting

This is a sample of
my handwriting

This is a Sample
of my handwriting

This is a sample
of my handwriting

This is a sample of my
hand writing

Jack

This is a sample of my
handwriting

This is
a sample
of my
hand writing

This is

This is a sample of
my handwriting

This is   a sample
of my handwriting .

Morton

this is a sample of
my handwriting

This is a sample of
My Handwriting

is a sample
writing.

This is a sample of
my handwriting

This is a sample of my handwriting

I know this is a sample of my handwriting.

This is a sample of my handwriting

This is a sample of my handwriting.

This is a of my h.

This is a sample of my handwriting

I know this of my hand

This is a sample of my handwriting

This is a of my hu

This is a sample of a sample
my Kadowitz. handwriting

This is a sample of This is a sample of
my handwriting my handwriting

This is a sample of my
handwriting

This is a sample of This is a sample of
my handwriting my handwriting

This is a Sample of samples
My handwriting my handwriting
like this

Jam This is a sample
of my handwriting.

This is a sample
of my handwriting

This is a x
of my hand

This is a sample of
my handwriting   sample

This is a Sample of

my Handwriting

This is a sample
of my hando

This is a sample of my
handwriting.

I know this is a sample of
my handwriting.

This is a
handwriting

I know this is
a sample of my
handwriting

This is a
Sample of
my handwriting

David

Jill

This is a sample of
my handwriting

This is a sample of
my handwriting

This is a Sample of my
Handwriting

This is a sample of my handwriting

Mr. Max.

This is a sample
of my handwriting

"Examine well your heads."

. . . Mikhail Naimy

> "Learn first to rule yourselves."
>
> . . . Mikhail Naimy

Mary Dawn Gladson

Mary Dawn Gladson says about herself and her work with graphoanalysis: "Anything I 'prescribed' for another I had already applied to myself through observing — and changing my writing. I experimented with myself, never with anyone else. For example, I adopted a number of different writing characteristics in order to *feel* what others feel who write that way. These episodes were brief and sometimes very uncomfortable.

"I found that making some changes were much more difficult than others. Resoluteness, however, really does pay-off. Daily I pay close attention to how I write and what I write in order to discover how I am truly feeling. It's amazing how revelatory — how accurate — our handwriting is, day by day. Once I *see* how I'm feeling, I can do something to right what I write and in doing so, I 'right' myself. What we fail to observe in our outer behavior confronts us from the piece of paper on which we inscribe our *inner* truth."

Mary's background is as vast as it is eclectic. She lectures widely, writes articles and plays (in some of which she performs) and has studied just about everything in order to "get better." What greater testimonial to her success than the woman herself? Direct, witty, ruthless and charming, her personality speaks from every page of this book. So does her knowledge and insight, a gift to the world from which all can benefit.

--- Daniel Whiteside